W9-AMZ-824

PHILOSOPHY AND LITERATURE

For Hege

PHILOSOPHY AND LITERATURE

An Introduction

Ole Martin Skilleås

Edinburgh University Press

© Ole Martin Skilleås, 2001

Edinburgh University Press Ltd
22 George Square, Edinburgh

Typeset in 11 on 13 pt Ehrhardt
by Hewer Text Ltd, Edinburgh, and
printed and bound in Great Britain by
MPG Books Ltd, Bodmin

A CIP Record for this book is
available from the British Library

ISBN 0 7486 1022 7 (paperback)

The right of Ole Martin Skilleås
to be identified as author of this work
has been asserted in accordance with
the Copyright, Designs and Patents Act 1988.

CONTENTS

FOREWORD

This book began its early life as lecture notes for an undergraduate course called 'Philosophy and Literature' in the Philosophy Department at Bergen University. During my two years at the English Department in Bergen I also taught a graduate course with the quizzical title 'Philosophy in Literature?'; and when I returned to the Philosophy Department I taught another graduate course called 'Literature in Philosophy?'. Students of all these courses have given me valuable feedback and have helped develop my own thinking during our discussions in and out of class. Two students in particular, Øystein Hide and Erik Tonning, deserve special mention since they read whole chapters in draft form and made very useful comments.

Because I was not able to find suitable introductory material for any of these courses, I decided to write my own. While doing this, I was fortunate to have the support and encouragement of several people. Professor Jeff Malpas, of the University of Tasmania, has been a long-distance inspirator and commentator. My debt to Professor Jeremy Hawthorn of the University of Trondheim goes back to my days as an undergraduate in English. An inspiring teacher and supervisor for my M.Phil. thesis, he also encouraged me to go to Britain to do a doctorate. Professor Stein Haugom Olsen, then at the University of Oslo, also helped me on my way, and has been very graceful in the face of my attempted criticisms of his work. He, together with Professor Peter Lamarque of the University of Hull, has been a source of inspiration and encouragement, and I have learnt a great deal from both over the years.

In Bergen, Marit Berge, of the English Department, has provided encouragement and inspiration, and so has my colleague Professor Kjell S. Johannessen, who pioneered philosophical studies of literature in Scandinavia. He also provided invaluable criticism on drafts of this book for which I am very grateful.

Since 1988, when I began work on my Ph.D. at the University of Warwick, I have benefited from close cooperation with Martin Warner. His immense knowledge and pioneering work in Philosophy and Literature has been of great use to me and others over the years. The following pages owe a great deal both to his inspiration and to his reading and constructive criticism of drafts of the book. All the remaining mistakes and shortcomings are, of course, my own.

Most of this book was written while suffering from sciatica, but my wife Hege remained the light of my life when everything else seemed bleak. This book is dedicated to her.

ONE

WHAT IS 'PHILOSOPHY AND LITERATURE'?

The question in the heading can clearly be answered in different ways. One such answer is that 'philosophy and literature' is just a conjunction of two subjects, no different as such from 'Sociology and Chemistry', or 'Psychology and Physics'. This is a view I do not share. Historically, philosophy can be seen to be the 'mother-subject' from which all other subjects have developed. The ancient philosophers speculated about almost anything, and the birth of the various subjects we know, like Mathematics, Physics, Economics and so on, all happened from within philosophy, whereby a separate methodology, in most cases based on empirical evidence, was developed, then widely accepted. Thus, a field of investigation was established. Psychology is a recent example of this process, and linguistics perhaps the most recent. Literature, however, is not a field of investigation and study in the same way as these. As an academic subject it is very recent; when Plato's Socrates[1] said that poetry[2] had been engaged in an 'ancient quarrel' with philosophy,[3] he did not have an academic subject in mind, of course, but the production and dissemination of literature.

Plato (c. 429–347 BC) is a central figure both in philosophy as such, and in its relationship with literature, and we will come back to him more fully in the next chapter. Suffice it to say here that he does his utmost to give poets and rhapsodes[4] a bad reputation, while composing his dialogues in such a sophisticated manner that one may well conclude that Plato himself was a master of the arts he so thoroughly criticised.[5] This double aspect – philosophy as exhibiting some of the most powerful traits of literature, and philosophy as competing with literature – makes an investigation into the interrelations of these two fields a fascinating endeavour.

Why, then, should Plato want to claim an ancient animosity between philosophy and literature? It is arguable that it was Plato who constituted philosophy as a separate undertaking, and keeping this in mind it is not surprising that he has so little to say in favour of poets and rhapsodes: he

1

had a need to put as much distance between literature and philosophy as possible. Small wonder he has Socrates claim that there was an ancient quarrel, for few quarrel more intensely than those with a rival claim to the same territory.[6]

Obviously, being in the same neighbourhood does not imply identity, and when you move into this neighbourhood you can approach it from several directions. In what follows I want to show that the two phenomena of philosophy and literature are entwined, and that the conjunction of the two constitutes a field of study. Doing this I have taken inspiration from the American philosopher Arthur C. Danto who in 1984 gave a talk for the American Philosophical Association with the title 'Philosophy as/ and/of Literature',[7] and I am going to use the possibilities of this title, with some modifications, as my sub-divisions of the rest of this chapter.

PHILOSOPHY AS LITERATURE

'Philosophy and Literature' can investigate the rhetoric[8] of philosophy, or 'philosophy *as* literature', in a manner of speaking. This is an area which has attracted renewed interest in recent years. It may be argued that discussions about the interrelations of philosophy and literature are in need of clear definitions of the two, but whether such are possible to arrive at, and what they could be, must be left for later chapters. Here we can only attempt a preliminary charting of the waters.

Danto puts 'philosophy as literature' in opposition to 'philosophy as science', where the latter has been an ideal for most of those who have practised philosophy in the analytic tradition in the twentieth century. Analytic philosophy, in its various guises, has established an ideal of clarity and precision in philosophy that Danto claims it has taken from the sciences. Since philosophy deals with some of the most intractable questions known to humanity, this is an aim worth pursuing. It serves no good purpose to serve up difficult arguments and discussions in a haze of impenetrable sentences and incomprehensible jargon. On the other hand there is the danger of simplification. That philosophy should be suited to clear and precise language is in itself a philosophical position by no means shared by all. Some may judge that the ideal of clarity makes for simplified and naive philosophy, which is therefore not adequate to the difficulty at the very heart of the subject. Some would even go so far as to claim that difficult texts may entice the reader to actively enter the discussion, that the difficulty of the text is a mirror image of the difficulty of thinking, and that the strain on the reader's ability to comprehend is only par for the course.

Such difficulties, however, will not by themselves make the text literary. Just as literature contains genres such as poetry, novels, plays and so on, and even sub-genres within these, philosophy has its genres as well. In this context it is important to remember that philosophy as an academic discipline became very professionalised during the twentieth century or so. It is arguable that this professionalisation has been instrumental in narrowing the range of genres by means of establishing criteria of professional advancement in terms of theses and publications, chiefly in the form of the refereed article.[9] It is arguable that this leads to uniformity and in some cases to rather boring reading, neither of which are conducive to philosophical reflection.

Fortunately, we have the whole of the history of philosophy at our disposal when examining philosophy as literature. It is not clear, however, what we are to mean by 'philosophy as literature'. In what sense, then, can you say that philosophy *is* literature? It cannot be sufficient that philosophy is also written, for so is the phone-book and any shopping list as well. It is, however, worth pointing out that works of philosophy are, whether they are dialogues, treatises, or an article in a journal, constructed so as to convince the reader of the truth of what is being proposed, and that the philosopher uses various forms of persuasion to reach this objective. All too often, though, readers may approach a work of philosophy in order to identify the arguments and their structure, while overlooking the way in which they are constructed and how the reader may be manipulated into accepting the propositions put forward by the author. The risk involved in this kind of practice is that you may be manipulated into accepting unfounded claims, or alternatively that you are not being open to forms of persuasion that cannot be boiled down to the bare bones of the argument. The latter risk is not the least.

One line of division between philosophy and literature widely held is that in the latter category we find fictional characters and situations, while philosophy is conducted in straight prose. Plato's dialogues prove the contrary, and show forms of persuasion that are not carried solely by the arguments put forward. In the dialogue *Phaedrus*, to which we shall return in Chapter 6, we see the characters Socrates and Phaedrus in conversation, and this conversation also constitutes the dialogue since there is no outside narrator. Socrates did exist, and it is probable that Phaedrus did as well, but we can be quite sure that this conversation never took place. From the moment the two of them meet in the first lines of the dialogue, until they unite in prayer and part ways in the last, this is pure fiction and at the same time one of the foundations of western philosophy. Much of what happens between the characters cannot be characterised as arguments for a proposition or hypothesis. Phaedrus may justifiably be seen as a somewhat hollow, if enthusiastic, character whose highest wish is to hear speeches and be enthused by these. When Socrates meets him outside Athens Phaedrus has been practising reciting a speech by Lysias, a famous rhetorician of the day. In this way, Phaedrus is portrayed as a representative of an unphilosophical approach to rhetoric. The way he acts in the dialogue also makes him seem a little ridiculous. A modern reader may well associate the way he wants to perform the speeches of their master with how Elvis impersonators dress up like their master and mime to a playback. Hardly any of this can be presented as arguments leading to a conclusion, but it clearly influences one's attitude to the disagreements between Socrates and Phaedrus.

The examples from Plato's dialogues can be multiplied, but the most important lesson to be learnt is that these genres are not in every way mutually exclusive. When one of the most widely used translations of Plato's *Phaedo* opens the preface with the words 'this book is designed for philosophical study of the *Phaedo*',[10] the presupposition is that the literary and the philosophical aspects of Plato can be separated with little or no loss. I believe that this kind of approach does not take Plato seriously, and misses aspects central and vital to his outlook and philosophy. *Phaedo* was written in the wake of the great epoch of Greek tragedy, and has a right to be valued as a drama as well as a philosophical treatise.[11]

That philosophy could benefit from reading its own texts with an eye for more than the geometric structure of its arguments does not only apply to such clear examples as the dialogues of Plato.[12] When the American philosopher Daniel Dennett warns against uncritical use and reading of what he calls 'intuition-pumps',[13] he does so against the use in philosophy of hypothetical examples and thought experiments. These are quite widespread despite the constraints imposed by academic publishing, and you may suspect that you are actually reading science-fiction when philosophers go on about split brains, Twin-Earth, possible worlds, Chinese rooms (examples from mainstream analytic philosophy in recent years). The point about these 'intuition-pumps' is not to dress up strict arguments that prove the conclusion from clearly stated premises, but to generate in the reader imaginative reflections that ultimately yield, not a formal conclusion, but an intuitive grasp of what is at issue.[14]

Philosophy in its written form is also subject to the demands we place on written accounts as such, and one such central demand is that these should be stimulating and comprehensible. In both philosophy and in literature it is sometimes pointed out that fantasies can be taken too far. One author who has been at the receiving end of such criticism is Doris

Lessing, who with her books in the series *Canopus in Argos: Archives* moved into the genre of science-fiction, or what she claims to belong to the genre of 'inner-space fiction'. To answer her critics, I suppose, she writes this in the introduction to the third novel in the series, *The Sirian Experiments*:

> What *of course* I would like to be writing is the story of the Red and White Dwarves and their Remembering Mirror, their space rocket (powered by anti-gravity), their attendant entities Hadron, Gluon, Pion, Lepton, and Muon, and the Charmed Quarks and the Coloured Quarks.
> But we can't all be physicists.[15]

What Lessing is getting at here is that accounts of the 'hardest' scientific results in particle physics and astronomy also use metaphors and allusions to other areas of experience, and that these do not seem any less fantastic than the fictions she presents in her own series of science-fiction novels. This goes for philosophy as well. Even the most abstract and precise of thoughts need narratives to be communicated effectively, but does that turn philosophy into literature? Hardly, and certainly no more than it turns particle physics into literature. It is a false construction to posit philosophy and literature as opposite domains from the opposition between literal and metaphorical language. We have seen already that the language of philosophy is also rhetorical – it cannot *but* be rhetorical, because it seeks to persuade, and rhetoric is the art of persuasion. Even if philosophy is not literature, it is of crucial importance for philosophy as such that it should be subject to the kind of analyses that are usually applied to literature. As we have seen already, the rationality of what is proposed may not be independent of how it is presented.

We have now reached the point where I think we can say with some degree of confidence that what I have decided to call 'philosophy as literature', analyses of the rhetorical and stylistic aspects of philosophy, is a field which, with some notable exceptions,[16] has been neglected, but which promises to be fruitful. This does not mean, however, that philosophy is the same as literature. Even if philosophy also uses traits we recognise from literature, we still distinguish between them.

LITERATURE AS PHILOSOPHY

If philosophy is not literature, could literature still be philosophy? One reason for posing such a question, in spite of the discussion above, is that many philosophers have also written works of an ostensibly literary nature, but still with obvious philosophical pretensions. One of these is the Danish philosopher Søren Kierkegaard, who under various pseudonyms and in different styles wrote works such as *The Diary of the Seducer*, which is clearly identifiable as a work of literature. Friedrich Nietzsche wrote *Thus Spoke Zarathustra*, which at least must be characterised as a very peculiar work of philosophy, if not a work of literature. Even prior to the nineteenth century philosophers wrote works which we could classify as literature today, such as St Augustine's *Confessions*. As pointed out above, however, there was more variety with respect to genres prior to the current professionalisation of philosophy.

In the twentieth century there are many examples of philosophers writing novels and poetry, or of authors philosophising. The French existentialists Albert Camus and Jean-Paul Sartre are famous examples, but this crossing of the boundaries (if such they are) is not confined to continental philosophers. In Britain, Iris Murdoch, who was a prize-winning author, was also a prominent philosopher.[17] Some philosophers have found that in trying to explain some point of philosophical importance, they have ended up writing novels, because unlike the dry prose of the philosophical paper, writing fiction does allow for the detail and circumstance of the lives we live, and to which the philosophy should have relevance.[18] What these examples show is that categorisation does not do justice to the variety of works written, and that probably goes for most fields. They do not show, however, that literature and philosophy are useless categories.

More often, however, one comes across claims that authors who have not produced writings of an ostensibly philosophical kind, or who do not address audiences expecting discussions of philosophy, 'have a philosophy' or in their fictions 'do philosophy'. One such example is the Polish-British author Joseph Conrad, who by some critics is said to have had a conservative philosophy of human society. Most readers interested in literature should also be familiar with claims such that Shakespeare in *King Lear* explores concepts such as 'self-insight' and 'trust'. This kind of interpretation was ridiculed by Richard Levin with the following fictional conversation between Ben Johnson and William Shakespeare in a Bankside tavern:

> B.J.:   What have you been doing lately, Will?
> W.S.:   I've been working on a new play.
> B.J.:   Oh, what will it be about?
> W.S.:   It will be a sustained meditation on reality and illusion.[19]

Some of the background for claims that authors have a philosophy may be the fact that philosophy and literature share a concern for the great and small truths of human existence. Aristotle (384–322 BC) famously said in his *Poetics* that poetry was closer to philosophy than is history, because 'poetry tends to speak of universals'.[20] That philosophy and literature should be seen to be polar opposites, particularly by analytic philosophers whose main stock in trade is conceptual analysis, may be due to rival claims to the truth. Philosophers of this persuasion may well feel that their approach to the big questions is more rational and that it clarifies the issues, and thus produces more insight than an author's entertaining play with purely fictional characters and situations. From their perspective, literary examples are threats to the clarity of thought.[21] Other philosophers, however, may share the view of Morris Weitz, who argues in *Philosophy in Literature* that philosophy and literature can enrich each other. He shows how literature aesthetically assimilates and transmits philosophy, and how philosophical themes contribute to the structural unity of the works he examines.[22]

Thus, it may rather be *the way* the major questions of human existence are approached that makes it sensible to talk about a difference between philosophy and literature, but that they share many of the same interests is quite obvious. An author, implied or real, may have an attitude to what he or she represents, or may write it with the intention of putting forward views on questions also being discussed in philosophy. One clear example of this would be an allegory where philosophical positions could take a human (or animal) shape, and could thus 'argue' for or against different positions. This is a marginal phenomenon, however. It is more usual that a reader interprets a work to be about something or other, call it a 'theme', or maybe several themes. Whether it is the reader, an implied or a real author who is responsible for the resulting interpretation is not the most important question in this context. What is interesting with regard to the question of whether literature can be philosophy is that literature may deal with some of the same questions as philosophy, but that the way these questions are approached makes it sensible to talk about separate spheres for philosophy and literature, despite the fact that there are grey areas between the two.

The American philosopher Stanley Cavell has made major contributions to what we can call 'literature as philosophy', particularly in his readings of Shakespeare's plays, most of which are published in his *Disowning Knowledge: in Six Plays of Shakespeare*.[23] As the title indicates it is particularly the thematic of scepticism that Cavell sees in some of Shakespeare's plays, and the perceptiveness of his readings forms a powerful argument – against the jibe from Richard Levin above – for the fruitfulness of philosophical readings of old plays. We shall leave a fuller discussion of Cavell for Chapter 7, but in an introduction to the field it is worth noting what he has to say about the interest of his approach. Cavell insists that Shakespeare could not be thought to be the greatest writer of the language 'unless his writing is engaging the depth of the philosophical preoccupations of his culture'.[24] Cavell works on the intuition that the scepticism that found its philosophical refinement in Descartes is already at work in Shakespeare's plays, and that both the philosophical and the literary modes are proper expressions of it.

Cavell's epistemological thematic is not the only ground common to philosophy and literature. Some claim that literature is the best way of investigating and shedding light on the complexity of ethical problems, and how they relate to personality and the particular situations in which the problems are situated. One of those is Martha Craven Nussbaum who in several works, particularly *Love's Knowledge*, argues such a view. Others, with sometimes rather different positions on ethical questions, such as Richard Eldridge, also argue the importance of literary examples for ethical matters.[25] As with Cavell, to do justice to these writers requires the space of a full chapter. However, some of the more basic questions relating to literature as philosophy should be posed now, so as to give an idea of what is to come.

There are, of course, problems relating to this field. If an interpreter, whether philosopher or not, finds a literary work to contain important insights, these insights may be ascribed to the author, to an implicit author, or even to the interpreter. The insights are, if they are particular to literature or even to one work, put forward in a literary form. In this case to boil them down to identifiable arguments is to deprive them of their very nature. Also, there is the problem of how any counter-argument could be proposed. Should a new novel be written to counter the claims put forward by the interpreter – or should the same work be interpreted in a way countering the claims made by the first interpreter? Obvious answers to these questions seem to be absent. Another problem is connected with the relativity of interpretations. It is well known that literary works give rise to sometimes widely divergent interpretations, and this makes it highly problematic to say that a work is about this, but not about that. Disagreements in literary interpretation often have their roots in this phenomenon, and they may make it difficult to claim that a certain work is an excellent guide to moral insight, for instance.

Ultimately, the question of whether novels, plays and poems represent positions with respect to philosophical questions, as well as if and how literature can illuminate these, must be discussed with reference to examples. That a good number of the best minds have found literary works to illuminate philosophical problems should in itself be reason enough to examine the doubts expressed in the previous paragraph. This discussion will be resumed in Chapter 7, 'Philosophy in Literature?', below.

PHILOSOPHY OF LITERATURE

Much of this book will be devoted to the philosophy of literature. The assumptions I have made above regarding literature in general, and not least the nature of literary interpretation, can be discussed under this heading. It may be asked, though, if this is not what is known as 'literary theory', and best left to those at home in studies of literature? After all, those who practise literature, as authors, publishers or critics, may feel the need to discuss questions about the aims and methods of their own practice, so why cannot philosophers just leave them well alone?

Traditionally, there have been three sources of knowledge or theory about art and literature. Arguably the most important has been and still is aesthetics, which is a philosophical discipline dealing with the general questions about the nature of art and beauty, and also ontological, epistemological and evaluative questions with regard to art. In addition to this, a number of what we may call 'instruction manuals' on 'how to do art' have been published, such as Longinus' *Ars Poetica* and Boileau's *L'Art Poétique*. As the third traditional kind of theorising about the arts we have artistic manifestos on what art is and is not, and what art should do. The prime example of this is Tolstoy's *What is Art?*.[26] In our day, though, most university departments teaching literature have courses in literary theory, where different 'schools' of literary theory are presented, such as formalism, new criticism, structuralism, psychoanalysis and so forth. Something, therefore, should be said regarding the relationship between such literary theory and philosophy of literature.

The philosophy of literature goes back a long way. Even if this term was not used at the time, Plato's and Aristotle's writings about tragedy and poetry can usefully be seen as the starting points of this tradition, and in the next chapter these will be examined more closely. With the advent of Aesthetics through the seminal writings of Baumgarten in the eighteenth century,[27] questions regarding the evaluation and interpretation of works of art, including literature, have come together, and with Kant's third critique, *The Critique of Judgement*,[28] aesthetics was brought into the mainstream of philosophy.

Literary theory, however, is a development of the twentieth century. This is neither the place nor the context for attempting a history of literary theory, but I shall point to some general features in order to clarify the relationship between literary theory and what I have called philosophy of literature, and why these came to part company. My focus here will be on the anglophone part of the world.

A number of the different theories being studied in courses of literary theory can usefully be called developments in the philosophy of literature. In introductions to literary theory we can see, for instance, Roman Ingarden's work mentioned under the heading of something called 'reader response theory'. It is unlikely that Ingarden or any other contributor to thinking about literature prior to some time in the 1940s would think of themselves as writing 'literary theory', let alone 'reader response theory'. It is possible they would have had the category of 'poetics' in mind,[29] while the term 'literary theory', as we shall see, only came to prominence in the 1970s. Classification as 'literary theory' implicit in most courses of literary theory has been carried out retroactively, and this is one reason why it is artificial to construct 'literary theory' as a compartment separate from the philosophy of literature. The Norwegian literary aesthetician Stein Haugom Olsen constructs an opposition between literary theory on the one hand and literary aesthetics on the other in the final essay of his book *The End of Literary Theory*.[30] Here literary theory is defined as the invasion of ideologically committed and fatally under-argued approaches into the serious and considered thinking about literature going on under the heading of 'literary aesthetics'. This opposition serves a polemical purpose, but stands in the way of seeing the common origin and the possibilities of cross-fertilisation between the traditions.

Literary theory is not so much a distinct discipline as the result of a greater interest among practitioners of literary criticism of the 'why and wherefore', not to mention 'how', of their profession. We may need, therefore, to distinguish between on the one hand criticism of literary works inspired by diverse ideas about literature, society, the human psyche and so on, and theories about literature and its relationship with, for instance, reality, language and the human mind on the other hand. It is the latter which is of prime relevance to this book. Any separation between literary theory and the philosophy of literature is mainly grounded in historical processes internal to the academic world. I. A. Richards was a philosopher by training who took up one of the first teaching posts in English at Cambridge University, where the school of English was founded as late as 1917. His background made him interested in the questions of interpretation and evaluation, and his books[31] were influential in generating an interest in these questions among the fledgling profession of academic literary criticism. In America, it is fair to say that the publication of Wimsatt and Beardsley's 'The Intentional Fallacy'[32] in

1946 generated a high level of discussion of questions relating to the interpretation of literature, and Wellek and Warren's *The Theory of Literature* further fuelled this interest. The term 'literary theory' may have come into academic usage by degrees after the publication of their book in the late 1940s, but it was not before the radicalisation of the universities in the 1960s and 1970s that 'literary theory' came to refer to roughly the same range of phenomena and approaches as it refers to today, and took on a life of its own.

In Britain and America the new movements among students brought with them a greater interest in intellectual currents prevalent on the European continent, particularly the French receptions of psychoanalysis and marxism. Marxism was a key inspiration for the new generation, but Karl Marx himself wrote very little about literature. The marxist Georg Lukács and his work on modernism had been studied for some time, though. Marxism and psychoanalysis, coupled with the traditions in linguistics from Ferdinand de Saussure, gave France a ferment of radical thought about literature which came into academia with the new generation of students – the post-war boom generation. First in America, then gradually – if reluctantly – in Britain, these movements led to a greater emphasis on theory in the studies of literature, and to courses in literary theory. In Britain these came to be taught first in the new universities established in the 1960s, and in North America it tended also to be the more marginal and less established universities that first offered courses in literary theory.

Feminism belongs in this picture, and was perhaps the most revolutionary and wide-ranging social and political movement of the twentieth century. Its impact on the study of literature is felt not only in conjunction with the movements already mentioned, but on a broad front and from critics of literature of most political and philosophical persuasions. As Cheri Register points out: 'feminist criticism is ultimately cultural criticism'.[33]

The present orientation around 'schools' in most courses on literary theory, however, has lost sight of the history of the fundamental questions relating to literature. Philosophy of literature, or literary aesthetics, is a branch of philosophy in close proximity to other areas of philosophy, such as the philosophy of language, epistemology, hermeneutics, metaphysics and the philosophy of mind. This gives the philosophy of literature considerable conceptual resources, and puts it in an intellectual setting where the standards of argumentation are high. Part of the purpose of this book is to introduce the philosophy of literature to those who study and care about literature, and thus to widen the scope of 'literary theory'.

There is little use for me to explain here what this area of philosophy contains, for major parts of this book will *show* what philosophy of literature is and what it can provide in the way of clarification of the phenomenon of literature and its relation to philosophy, though it cannot be exhaustive in its treatment of problems from this field. My *foci* in the philosophy of literature will be the definition of literature, the authority of the author and the nature of literary interpretation. I propose, however, to start at the beginning of this long tradition of philosophising about literature, which also provides the starting point both for 'philosophy as literature' and 'literature as philosophy'. Plato wanted to banish the poets and the rhapsodes from his ideal republic, and thus started a debate about the nature and value of literature that will certainly not be over with the end of this book.

FURTHER READING

In addition to *books* mentioned in the Notes, there is a collection worth mentioning which shows the quality and variety of contributions to this field: *Philosophy and Literature*, edited by A. Phillips Griffiths, Royal Institute of Philosophy Lecture Series: 16 (Cambridge: Cambridge University Press, 1984).

In *Inconvenient Fictions: Literature and the Limits of Theory* (New Haven, CT: Yale University Press, 1991), Bernard Harrison not only attempts to reconcile deconstruction and humanism, but he also argues that literature is valuable because it has the ability to challenge our mental configurations, as well as recondition our sluggish moral responses.

There are also a number of journals with contributions to the field of philosophy and literature. Chief among these, perhaps, is the journal *Philosophy and Literature*, sponsored by Whitman College and distributed by Johns Hopkins University Press, Baltimore. It comes out twice a year, and is edited from the United States and New Zealand. *Philosophy and Literature* publishes philosophical interpretations of literature, literary investigations of classic works of philosophy as well as articles on the aesthetics of literature, and philosophy of language relevant to literature.

Journals of general aesthetics almost always publish articles and book reviews relevant to philosophy and literature. Two of the best known are *The British Journal of Aesthetics*, published quarterly by Oxford University Press, Oxford, for The British Society of Aesthetics, and *The Journal of Aesthetics and Art Criticism*, also quarterly, but by The American Society for Aesthetics, at the University of Wisconsin-Madison and Marquette University.

Articles about philosophy and literature can be found in a wide variety of journals, but two others deserve special mention: *New Literary History*, published three times a year by Johns Hopkins University Press, Baltimore, and *Critical Inquiry*, quarterly, by Chicago University Press, Chicago.

Finally, David E. Cooper (ed.), *A Companion to Aesthetics* (Oxford: Blackwell, 1992) contains a number of succinct articles which are relevant to many of the issues discussed in this book.

NOTES

1. Socrates (c. 470–399 BC) did not write anything himself, and the reason I distinguish between the person Socrates, and Plato's use of Socrates in many of his dialogues, is that the latter is a character who may or may not express beliefs similar to those of the person Socrates, who was dead by the time Plato wrote his dialogues.
2. Plato and his contemporaries wrote about 'poetry' where we, with a wider range of recognised genres, would use 'literature'. In the following I shall use 'literature' when this wider sense is intended, but stick to 'poetry' and 'poets' in quotations and when the specific genre is in question.
3. Plato, *The Republic*, book X, 607b.
4. The word 'rhapsode' means, literally, 'someone who joins together songs'. It is derived from *rhaptein*, which means 'to join together', and *ode*, which originally means 'song'. Rhapsodes performed literary works, often by Homer, at festivals.
5. An introduction to these questions can be found in G. R. F. Ferrari, 'Plato and Poetry', in George A. Kennedy (ed.), *The Cambridge History of Literary Criticism: Volume 1 – Classical Criticism* (Cambridge: Cambridge Univeristy Press, 1989), pp. 92–148.
6. Some people have suggested a cease-fire on this front, and claim that these fields are really quite different even if they seem similar. See Stein Haugom Olsen, 'Thematic Concepts: Where Philosophy Meets Literature', in *The End of Literary Theory* (Cambridge: Cambridge University Press, 1987), pp. 176–95.
7. Arthur C. Danto, 'Philosophy and/as/of Literature', in Anthony J. Cascardi (ed.), *Literature and the Question of Philosophy* (Baltimore, MD: Johns Hopkins University Press, 1987), pp. 3–23.
8. Rhetoric is the art of speaking and writing well; the skill of addressing people so as to influence their minds. In antiquity Plato set philosophy up to be the antithesis of rhetoric as practised in his day by the so-called sophists. His main argument was that the sophists used their rhetorical skills to persuade, rather than to seek the truth. Philosophy, on the other hand, was a search for the truth.
9. This means that the article is made anonymous by the journal and sent out to

two experts in the subject. These two, independently of each other, decide whether or not the article is worthy of publication.

10. Plato, *Phaedo*, trans. David Gallop (Oxford: Oxford University Press, 1975), p. v.

11. See Martin Warner, *Philosophical Finesse: Studies in the Art of Rational Persuasion* (Oxford: Clarendon Press, 1989), pp. 67–104, for a study on the interrelations of literary and philosophical aspects of the *Phaedo*.

12. Plato is not the only philosopher to have written dialogues. We know that Aristotle did, though none of his have survived to our time. Berkeley wrote his *Three Dialogues between Hylas and Philonous* (1713), and Hume wrote *Dialogues Concerning Natural Religion* (1779), to name but two of the better known examples.

13. Daniel Dennett, 'The Milk of Human Intentionality', *Behavioural and Brain Sciences*, 3 (1980), pp. 428–30, and also later in *The Mind's I: Fantasies and Reflections on Mind and Soul* (New York: Basic Books, 1981), ed. with Douglas R. Hofstadter, and *Elbow Room* (Oxford: Oxford University Press, 1984).

14. Dennett, *Elbow Room*, p. 12.

15. Doris Lessing, *The Sirian Experiments* (London: Granada, 1982), p. 12.

16. One prominent exception is Berel Lang, see for instance *The Anatomy of Philosophical Style: Literary Philosophy and the Philosophy of Literature* (Oxford: Blackwell, 1990).

17. Some of her better known novels are *The Black Prince*, *The Sea, The Sea*, and *The Philosopher's Pupil* (Published in London by Chatto & Windus, in 1973, 1978 and 1983 respectively), while her philosophical writings include *The Sovereignty of Good* (London: Routledge, 1970) and *Metaphysics as a Guide to Morals* (London: Chatto & Windus, 1992).

18. One example of this happening is the Norwegian Professor of Philosophy Jon Hellesnes, who ended up writing the novel *Carolus, klovnen: Roman* (Oslo: Gyldendal, 1982) (in English: *Carolus, the Clown: Novel*, but not translated into English) when trying to prepare a paper for a conference.

19. Richard Levin, *New Readings vs. Old Plays* (Chicago, IL: University of Chicago Press, 1979), p. 17.

20. The *Poetics* has been translated into a number of different languages, and in a wide variety of editions. I have used Aristotle, *Poetics: with the 'Tractatus Coislinianus', reconstruction of 'Poetics II', and the fragments of 'On Poets'*, trans. Richard Janko (Indianapolis, IN: Hackett, 1987), 51b7. This translation will be used in this book, and references given in the main text. Janko deletes the first two digits of Bekker's pagination in his edition of Aristotle's works from 1830, so the quotation above is translated from page 1451 of Bekker's edition, part b (of the page), and line 7 of this. Of course, it is nearly impossible to make translations correspond exactly to the lines of the original. Typographical marks in Janko's text referring to sources have been deleted by me.

21. Examples of this way of thinking can be found in R. M. Hare, *Moral Thinking* (Oxford: Oxford University Press, 1981), pp. 47–9, and C. W. K. Mundle, *A Critique of Linguistic Philosophy* (Oxford: Oxford University Press, 1970), p. 14. Then there are others, who like Richard Rorty in *Consequences of Pragmatism* (Brighton: Harvester Press, 1982) sees philosophy only as a kind of writing, and thus more similar to literature. See particularly Rorty's essay 'Philosophy as a Kind of Writing: An Essay on Derrida', pp. 90–109.

22. Morris Weitz, *Philosophy in Literature: Shakespeare, Voltaire, Tolstoy, and Proust* (Detroit, MI: Wayne State University Press, 1963).

23. Stanley Cavell, *Disowning Knowledge: in Six Plays of Shakespeare* (Cambridge: Cambridge University Press, 1987).

24. Cavell, *Disowning Knowledge*, p. 2.

25. Martha Craven Nussbaum, *Love's Knowledge: Essays on Philosophy and Literature* (Oxford: Oxford University Press, 1990). Also *The Fragility of Goodness: Luck and Ethics in Greek Tragedy and Philosophy* (Cambridge: Cambridge University Press, 1986). Richard Eldridge, *On Moral Personhood: Philosophy, Literature, Criticism, and Self-Understanding* (Chicago, IL: University of Chicago Press, 1989). Frank Palmer, *Literature and Moral Understanding* (Oxford: Clarendon, 1992). Political philosophy has also given more attention to the study of literature lately, see for instance the collection *Literature and the Political Imagination*, John Horton and Andrea T. Baumeister (eds) (London: Routledge, 1996).

26. Leo Tolstoy, *What is Art? and Essays on Art*, trans. Aylmer Maude (Oxford: Oxford University Press, 1930).

27. Alexander Gottlieb Baumgarten, *Texte zur Grundlegung der Ästhetik*, ed. H. R. Schweizer (Hamburg: Felix Meiner Verlag, 1983) and *Theoretische Ästhetik: Die grundlegenden Abschnitte der 'Aesthetica'*, ed. H. R. Schweizer (Hamburg: Felix Meiner Verlag, 1983). The *Aesthetica* was first published in Frankfurt in 1750.

28. Immanuel Kant, *The Critique of Judgement*, trans. Werner S. Pluhar (Indianapolis, IN: Hackett, 1987). The title of the original of 1790 is *Kritik der Urteilskraft*.

29. For René Wellek and Austin Warren in their *Theory of Literature* (London: Jonathan Cape, 1949), 'poetics' was co-extensive with 'literary theory' (p. v), while 'the term "theory of literature" might well include – as this book does – the necessary "theory of literary criticism" and "theory of literary history"' (p. 30). Their concept was therefore wider than the usage current today.

30. Stein Haugom Olsen, *The End of Literary Theory* (Cambridge: Cambridge University Press, 1987), pp. 196–211.

31. Some of his numerous publications include: *The Meaning of Meaning: A Study of the Influence of Language upon Thought and of the Science of Symbolism*, with C. K. Ogden, 3rd edn. (London: Kegan Paul, 1930), first

published 1923; *Principles of Literary Criticism* (London: Kegan Paul, 1926), first published 1924; *Practical Criticism: A Study of Literary Judgement* (London: Routledge, 1929).

32. Reprinted in W. K. Wimsatt, *The Verbal Icon: Studies in the Meaning of Poetry* (Lexington, KY: University Press of Kentucky, 1954). First published in 1946, in *Sewanee Review*.

33. Cheri Register, 'American Feminist Literary Criticism: A Bibliographical Introduction' in Josephine Donovan (ed.), *Feminist Literary Criticism: Explorations in Theory* (Lexington, KY: University Press of Kentucky, 1975), p. 10.

TWO

PHILOSOPHY AND LITERATURE IN ANTIQUITY

If you pick up two different translations of a text from ancient Greece of nearly 2500 years ago you will see how different they are. Your first reaction may be that one or possibly both of the translators are incompetent since the translations are so divergent, but the reason is probably that there are major problems of translating these texts into modern languages. Not only do we have to reconstruct the Greek of the time, which is notoriously difficult, but the writers also sometimes had very different ideas from us as to what the world was really like. They had a different 'world picture' from us. In dealing with these problems the translator has to choose a strategy. One strategy is to emphasise writing a clear, fluent and consistent target language, and an alternative is to sacrifice these ideals in favour of a translation more faithful to the original, translating more or less 'word by word'. Of course, most try to combine the two, but in different proportions.

At the time when Plato and Aristotle lived, probably nobody read texts silently. St Augustine in his *Confessions*, notes with surprise that Ambrose, the Bishop of Milan, reads silently, but that was more than half a millennium later. He was not the first to do so, other isolated instances have been noted, but silent reading did not become usual in the west until the tenth century AD.[1] plato and aristotle's contemporaries held beliefs very different from ours about the world we live in, and we should be careful not to think that we can easily enter their minds. we must reconstruct not only the words of these texts with great care, knowing that the concepts of the ancient greeks were often very different from ours, but we must also be conscious of a tendency in ourselves to assume that they were 'really like us'.

PLATO (c.429–347 BC)

We need to take care also when we approach the relationship between philosophy and literature in antiquity again. As we saw in the previous

17

chapter, Plato refers to an 'ancient quarrel' between literature and philosophy,[2] and we may wonder what his motivation was for concerning himself with questions relating to philosophy and literature.[3] A possible answer is that he wants to establish philosophy as the discourse of knowledge by separating it as clearly as possible from literature – a discourse too evocative and passionate to allow philosophical reason and rationality to dominate.[4] The quarrel can be seen to be between literature and the emotions on the one side, and philosophy and rationality on the other. Plato's preferred discourse was rational argumentation, so there can be no doubt about which side he was on. He advocated 'dialectic', a term which has come to have different meanings during the history of western philosophy, but for our purposes the Socratic sense should suffice: it is discussion by means of question and answer, in order to define or examine a concept or phenomenon. Having established a way to discover the truth, he may have set out to discredit other and more established competitors. Given this picture, we may understand his negative view of literature, which, as we shall see, was indeed a close competitor in classical Greek culture.

What was Plato's philosophy, if any? This question may sound disingenuous, but it is not. His writings were in the form of dialogues, with two or more interlocutors, but Plato was never one of them. A character called Socrates turns up in many of them, and in all of the earlier ones. We are quite sure that Plato was influenced by the real-life Socrates, who never wrote anything but acted almost like an intellectual *agent provocateur* in Athens when Plato was young. Socrates was sentenced to death, and we think that Plato then resolved to continue Socrates' work. We should not, however, assume that the Socrates of the dialogues really is the mouthpiece of Plato, even though many philosophers and others do.[5] In later dialogues Socrates disappears, only to turn up again once, in *Philebus*, and a possible reason for his disappearance is that the 'method' of the dialogues changes. In earlier dialogues the method is for Socrates to ask someone who is presumed to be an expert, or at least to be in a particular position to answer, what the meaning is of a general concept. In *Hippias Major*, Socrates asks Hippias what beauty is. Several answers are provided by Hippias, but none of them prove satisfactory. Then the same question is pursued by Socrates himself, thinly disguised as a person Socrates once met. However, the result is still unsatisfactory, and Socrates concludes that beauty is a very difficult thing. This progression is quite typical of the earlier dialogues, while in the middle dialogues, such as the *Symposium* and the *Republic*, a more systematic philosophy is proposed, but still always through characters in the dialogue. It is from the middle dialogues that most views of what was Plato's philosophy are constructed. In Plato's later dialogues, however, characters sometimes present severe criticism of what was proposed in the middle dialogues. We cannot know why this is, but some think that Plato changed his views and that the later dialogues represent a development in his thinking. Others have suggested that all the dialogues were perhaps only thought-experiments, and mainly designed to provoke readers to continue the discussions in the dialogues, and to think for themselves.[6] In any case, a brief outline of the consensus view of Plato's philosophy in his middle period will help us understand his views on the relationship between philosophy and literature.

According to what we think Plato believed, we humans live in a world which is only a poor copy of an ideal world beyond what we can sense. This is a realm of non-perceptible objects which are variously called 'ideas' or 'forms'. This realm is the only strictly real one, and the only one about which we can have any knowledge. In a previous existence we had access to this ideal world, but when thrown into this one we forgot. The objects and phenomena we can sense in this existence are only, in some sense, copies of the forms. We can, however, be reminded of the realm of ideas through various means. In the dialogue *Phaedrus*, which we shall examine in Chapter 6, 'beauty' is presented as the form which it is easiest to be reminded of because sight is the keenest sense we have. However, the main way to knowledge of the really existing objects is through rational clarification of the key concepts of our existence, such as truth and justice. These are all forms, but the form of the good is the key one, and the one which illuminates all the others. The full knowledge of the form of the good is the main aim of philosophy, and philosophers are to rule the ideal society by virtue of their special insights into the realm of forms. In the *Republic*, Plato also proposes an organisation of human society which is based on these views, and where the roles in society are distributed in accordance with which parts of their souls people are governed by. It is based on a psychology which maintains that the producers are governed by their appetites, and should produce, the soldiers are governed by their courage, and should guard the republic, and the ruling philosophers are, of course, governed by rationality.

It is no surprise, therefore, that Plato sided with reason against emotion. The emotions mess things up, and are diverse and unruly, while reason is unitary. Reason can connect human society with the stable and eternal perfection of the forms, and anything that upsets this should be stamped out. This, anyway, is the 'standard' view of Plato, a view which will be modified by our discussion both in this chapter and in

Chapter 6, 'Literature in Philosophy?'. However, the standard view may explain why the character of Socrates was so strongly opposed to literature whenever this phenomenon came up in discussions. Not only did literature appeal to and strengthen the anti-rational emotions, literature was in any case just a poor copy of the world of our senses, which in its turn is just a poor copy of the only really existing things: the unitary and enduring forms. Literature only takes us even further from reality, another feature of literature unlikely to appeal to Plato.

We must also remember, by the way, that ancient Greece did not have the concept 'literature'. What we would normally call literature is, in the texts we are going to examine here, usually referred to as 'poetry', except when Aristotle specifically writes about tragedy or epic. When the phenomenon being discussed in the following is not particular to any specific genre of literature, such as poetry or theatre, I shall use 'literature' to conform with present practice. In this context it is also important to note that literature in ancient Greece took different forms. Rhapsodes took turns to recite all of Homer during festivals lasting several days, and often there was a competitive element in the festivals. On the other hand we have the tragedies which have their roots in the Dionysus festivals, where *tragedia* in its origins was the passion of the god Dionysus. We cannot therefore say that literature in Greece at Plato's time was a tool for serious reflection, and this forms part of the background to Plato's attitude to literature. We shall now examine two of Plato's dialogues where most of his views on literature are presented.

ION

To get to grips with what Plato's agenda was we may look at his short and early dialogue *Ion*.[7] It is fair to say that Socrates' interlocutor, the rhapsode Ion, puts his foot in it in this dialogue. What he says does nothing for his credibility as an expert on his own profession, and Socrates does not pull any punches. These two characters, Ion and Socrates, are citizens of different cities, something that is brought up when Socrates in the first lines of the dialogue asks Ion if he has just arrived from his home town of Efesos. In virtue of their home towns they represent different ways of life. Ionians, and people from Efesos in particular, were considered by Athenians such as Plato to be emotional, effeminate and concerned with the appearance of things – in contrast with Athenians like Socrates, who were regarded, particularly by themselves, as more rigidly logical and intellectual. In a way, this is the well-known conflict between sense and sensibility, and Plato draws attention to it by introducing the provenance of the two characters.

This conflict is at the heart of Plato's quarrel with literature. At the beginning of the dialogue *Ion*, Socrates and Ion meet in Athens, and they start talking about Ion's skill as a rhapsode. Ion has won a competition for rhapsodes, and Socrates wants to know if he is equally adept at reciting all the poets. Ion is not: Homer is his speciality, and if any other author is being recited or talked about, Ion loses all interest and often falls asleep. Socrates claims that Ion's skills are not those of a profession or a craft, a *techne*, for then he would have been equally good at reciting all poets, and not just Homer. Socrates shows that all other artists are equally good at their art, no matter what the subject is, but that rhapsodes are not. Socrates claims that the skill of the rhapsodes is due to divine inspiration, and not to their craft. Ion, as a rhapsode, is just a link in a chain of inspiration originating with the gods. The comparison Socrates makes is with a magnetic stone under which one may hang a number of metallic rings, one below the other, and in just the same way the inspiration from the gods is transmitted through several instances, of which the rhapsode is just one. 'The lyric poets are not in their senses when they make these lovely lyric poems . . . for not by art do they utter these poems, but by power divine' (534a–c). The irony here is not to be missed, for these passages (533c–535) are the most beautiful and 'poetic' of the whole dialogue, and Socrates himself (or Plato writing it) seems to be inspired.

Ion is criticised because he has no particular skill or knowledge of the subjects he recites, but this is a criticism few would present against authors today. We should keep in mind, however, that poets and playwrights had a particular position in ancient Greek society. The Greeks in antiquity went to the poets, transmitted through the rhapsodes, to gain factual knowledge – particularly, but not only, about religious matters. Poets also had a major position in education, which we see in Plato's dialogue *Protagoras*.[8] Ion considers himself to be an expert on all the numerous subjects Homer says something about. So, tradition, factual knowledge and wisdom were transmitted from the poets (particularly Homer) by the rhapsodes. In this way rhapsodes, disseminating the work of the poets, were in direct competition with the philosophers. Therefore, Plato, as a philosopher, wanted to discredit poets and rhapsodes in order to accommodate the lovers of wisdom (the *philo-sophoi*).[9] The former were only mouthpieces for accepted and authoritative wisdom, while the philosophers were critical seekers of the truth.

In *Ion*, then, Socrates claims that rhapsodes have neither *techne* (practical skill) nor *episteme* (knowledge), but are possessed by a divine power (*theia dunamis*), and claims that this possession is incompatible with *techne*.[10] The rhapsodes are not the only ones possessed: all those who are parts of the transmission from the gods via the poets to the public are included. This is made clear from the fact that Plato uses the same concept, *legein*, both about poetic composition and about recitation, thus making them parallel activities in his account. In this process everybody is *enthousiazontes* (possessed by divinity), just as the magnetic stone transmits its power through the rings hanging from it. This possession, the *theia mania*, is transmitted to the audience through the emotional response of the rhapsode to what he is performing. Ion confirms this, and it is precisely the theatrical aspect, the lack of critical distance, that Plato reacts against. This may well be the core of Plato's opposition to poetry, poets, and those who perform poetry and thus transmit it to the audience. It seems that it is not only the poets' and the rhapsodes' lack of knowledge that is at fault, but also their ability to infect everybody with their irrational rapture. So, not only do they not have any knowledge to convey, but they make critical distance and rational debate impossible by the way they communicate.

In our day it is hard not to feel that Plato goes to war against highly valuable aspects of his own culture, such as Homer and the great dramatic works of the period, and that he is as wrong as he can be. We have to remember, however, that his culture was still primarily oral in its means of communication, to the extent that even the written was oral, for written material was read aloud. We understand that the private reader curled up in the comfy chair was still a long way off. It is important to keep this performance aspect in mind when we consider if he was right to condemn literature. It is quite clear that there was precious little chance of enjoying a critical distance at the poetry festivals, and no more at the Dionysus festivals, and it is precisely this critical distance which is so vital for the philosophical method as Plato conceived of it. For Plato the dialectic method was the key to true knowledge, and not the transmission of old knowledge through Homer, or the continued knowledge of the Gods through the performance of the tragedies.

If we look more closely at the performance aspect, we may see what Plato found to be so objectionable about literature. The performance of literature means that the creator of the work has withdrawn, only to leave the stage open for his creatures: the characters. These, in turn, are presented by other persons, the actors, or in the case of the rhapsode they are presented by a one-man band of different characters. The chorus and the characters compete over whose version of the events should be the defining one. In Homer's *Odyssey*, for instance, all the acts that are portrayed as being just appear to have nothing in common, and there is in any case no room to pause and reflect in order to arrive at any stable view of what justice is. Thus, through its own means of communication, literature insists on its own irreducible plurality with regard to reality. This means that there is no privileged voice to explain the deep unity of reality, which is at the heart of Plato's metaphysics. In the case of justice, for example, Plato held that there is a form, in a superior realm of existence, which is justice, and that all just actions share in this form. Literature, on the other hand, seems to demand our acceptance of an irreducible plurality, and Plato, of course, would not stand for it. This may explain his attacks on literature in *Ion* and in the *Republic*. The latter is our next candidate for examination.

THE REPUBLIC

Even if Plato seems to have changed his views throughout his long writing career, most commentators turn to the 'middle' dialogue, the *Republic*, as the main source of his views on most areas of philosophy. This dialogue offers an integrated vision of the ideal society, as well as developed arguments for positions on major questions in epistemology and metaphysics. A developed and nuanced view of Plato would have to mention how he may have changed his views on most of the matters discussed in the *Republic*, but that should not concern us here, for he does not directly contradict elsewhere the views on the relationships between philosophy and literature presented in this dialogue. This, in particular, makes the attack on poetry in Book 10 worrying for all but the most fundamentalist of the readers of today, and Plato uses all the means available to give poetry a bad press.

I shall try to show that this attack, just like the one presented in *Ion*, can only be understood against the background of the intellectual climate at the time, and that it is not an attack against present conceptions of literature or art.[11] In this way I hope to draw the lines from antiquity up to today on the important questions about 'the company we keep',[12] both with respect to literature, and to the other media.

Plato discusses literature, and its role in society, in earlier books of *The Republic*, but in books 2 and 3 the discussion centres around the role of literature in the education of the young protectors of the republic. Here literature has a role to play, but it is heavily controlled and curtailed. Only poets and story-tellers who are severe rather than amusing, and who portray the style of the good man, are allowed (398b) – as long as they do as they are told by those supervising the education, that is. In book 10 the topic is the total exclusion of literature, even if some hymns to the gods and higher-ranking citizens can be allowed (607a). Given the importance and popularity of the theatre and the Homer festivals, this radical exclusion must have been quite shocking to the average Athenian.

In books from 3 to 10 of the *Republic*, Plato develops his metaphysics, epistemology and psychology. However, the interpretation of such a dense and extensive dialogue as the *Republic* is always difficult. An example of this is that Socrates, at the beginning of book 10, says that all mimetic poetry has been excluded from the republic, while we can read in book 3 that he encourages the young to imitate the good persons portrayed in heroic poetry. However, Plato does not want to outlaw imitation, which he considers central to a good education, but *imitativity* – the desire and ability to imitate whatever, independent of its moral worth, and without the proper attitude. So when Socrates says that all mimetic poetry has been excluded from the republic, he does not refer to all imitation, but only to that poetry which encourages and leads to imitativity. The result is that if poetry is allowed, pleasure and pain will rule rather than law and the rational principles – commonly accepted to be the best (607a).

This may indicate that Plato is blind to the real values of art, but he is not concerned with art as such, and the reason is not that the concept of 'the fine arts' only came to notice with the Enlightenment. Neither painting nor sculpture were party to Plato's ban, and this makes it even more important to establish what it is about imitative poetry that makes it so dangerous. Plato says that this is because it is a medium particularly well suited for the imitation of vulgar subjects and shameful behaviour (604e). Even the best among us are vulnerable to such influence (605c–d), for when we are exposed to the overwhelming and exaggerated wailing and complaining which is the core of much tragic and epic poetry, we tend to share the feelings of the hero and praise the poet and the rhapsode who most strongly affects us with his representation (605d). However, it is just such behaviour we seek to avoid if we meet with misfortune in our own lives. In real life we praise control and not excessive emotion (605e).

Plato's answer to why we admire in poetry what we would feel ashamed of in real life lies in the tripartition of the soul introduced in book 4 of *The Republic*, between the rational, the courageous and the appetitive, or passionate, parts of the soul. Poetry presents the suffering of others, not our own, and the rational part of the soul gives free reign to the passions to express themselves in this context (606a–b). Nevertheless, encouraging such emotions in the theatre, or with the rhapsode, makes us more disposed to express them thus in our own case as well, and not to be ashamed of it. This in its turn make us more prone to make a spectacle of ourselves, to put it that way. Socrates generalises this to apply to all feelings (606d), and poetic imitation makes these grow when they really ought to wither and die.

Plato, therefore, accuses poetry of perverting its audience. In its very nature it is particularly suitable to represent 'low characters' and vulgar themes, and this is because such characters and themes are easy to imitate, and the mass audience wants to watch and listen. The real problem is that our own soul has a parallel to the mass: the appetitive part (580d–581a). Plato's most important assumption here is that our reactions to poetry are transferred directly on to, and determine, our reactions to situations in real life. Poetry, therefore, makes us react in ways we should really be ashamed of, and it institutes a bad government in the soul of each and every one of us. This is in clear and direct contradiction to the purpose of the republic, which is to foster the best part of the soul, and to make this part determine the course of society as a whole. So there is little wonder why Plato would want to banish literature from the republic; literature threatens its very purpose.

Plato assumes that our reactions to real-life events follow our reactions to literature and, superficially at least, it is easy to reject such an assumption. However, to react in this way is to misunderstand what is important about Plato's assumptions. If we consider the case of children, we may find what he says quite plausible. Most of us have found that children tend to imitate bad role-models. When we were small we were told not to imitate people with certain ticks or who were behaving oddly: 'you may become like that yourself' – and we stopped immediately (why take the risk?). Even as parents we may worry about this. Plato says that 'have you not noticed how dramatic and similar representations, if indulgence in them is prolonged into adult life, establish habits of physical poise, intonation and thought which become second nature' (395d). Aristotle agrees with Plato here, and suggests banning children from seeing certain kinds of representations.[13] A present-day parallel is the classification system for movies. Our reason for this and other similar measures, is that children often react to representations as if they were real. Plato believes the same is the case for adults. For him representation is translucent – it gets all its relevant properties, those that make it what it is, from what is being represented. In book 10 all representations are being treated as make-believe objects, and not as objects with a separate status. After all, as we saw in *Ion*, imitators do not have a *techne* – their own craft – and therefore they do not know the true nature of what they are imitating either. They just represent how it appears, and the easiest to represent, given their appeal to our emotions, are sex, violence and the dramatic. So what happens, in turn, is that people imitate such behaviour in their own lives.

Plato's view here seems to be the almost universal premise for the present debates about sex, violence and anti-social activities on film, video, TV, and most recently the Internet. As the literary critic Wayne C. Booth says, with the backing of innumerable others: 'as a viewer I become how I view . . . Unless we change their characteristic forms, the new media will surely corrupt whatever global village they create; you cannot build a world community on misshapen souls'.[14] Others assert that TV and other visual or compound media require minimal skill to comprehend, and aim for emotional and other gratification. Plato's fear of the masses seems still to be with us. The parallels with Plato are even more numerous than those mentioned already. According to experts on drama in ancient Greece,[15] the theatrical public were representative of the population as a whole. Pericles established the *theoreticon*, a subsidy which made it free to attend, and the audience could reach 17,000. It was a day out for most, with lots of food, booing and hissing. Contemporary stories said that pregnant women miscarried when the Furies of Aeschylus' *Eumenides* came on stage. We do not know whether this was true or not, but it is significant that it was believed at the time. The distinction between play and reality was blurred, and this formed the background to the views of Plato.

Then as now, the higher and educated levels of society were worried about the masses – that they should be corrupted by the representations they were exposed to, that they would copy in their own lives what they saw through these representations. Today the theatre, as well as poetry and other literature, has increasingly become the preserve of the educated middle and upper classes, while the broad masses turn to the new media, such as TV, videos and the Internet. These media are the true parallel to poetry and drama in Plato's own time, and we see the same kinds of concern among the intelligentsia as that shown by Plato himself two and a half millennia ago. All the way from antiquity, through the Renaissance and puritan England, through the attacks on the novel in the eighteenth century and later, popular entertainment has been accused of large-scale corruption and of mirroring a depraved and degrading reality. Aesthetics today almost completely neglects TV, and defends those forms of art our practices of interpretation have made innocuous. The point is that both Plato and many present-day critics believe that popular entertainment mirrors reality, while nobody today thinks that the fine arts do. Most informed people now would say that we understand literature through interpretations and transformations, and make it relevant to our lives, if at all, in ways more abstract than imitation. Seen thus, perhaps literature as we conceive of it today can escape Plato's criticism? He may have opened up for such an eventuality when he wrote:

> 'It is only fair, then, that poetry should return, if she can make her defence in lyric or other metre.'
>
> 'Yes.'
>
> 'And we should give her defenders, men who aren't poets themselves but who love poetry, a chance of defending her in prose and proving that she doesn't only give pleasure but brings lasting benefit to human life and human society. And we will listen favourably, as we shall gain much if we find her a source of profit as well as of pleasure.'
>
> *(The Republic,* 607d3–e2)

ARISTOTLE (384–322 BC)

Plato did not have to wait long for an answer. Aristotle, as a pupil and discussion-partner for Plato, must have known the passage above, and it is not unlikely that the *Poetics* is an answer to its invitation.[16] It is amusing, actually, that Socrates should say 'lyric or other metre' in the quotation. What we have left of Aristotle's writings are probably notes relating to his teaching, a genre not known for its lyrical beauty, so it is a good thing that Socrates allowed the defenders of poetry to use prose. Some parts of the *Poetics* were probably written at an early stage in his writing career, while others were added later. This is because it was a document used in Aristotle's own Lyceum, his school or college, and the texts, just like a lecturer's notes, were amended and added to over time. This makes it difficult to follow, and it does not improve matters that the original papyrus scrolls did not have sections, headings, capital letters and quite often no space between the words. The version we have today has been copied, and re-copied, by scribes through the centuries, and the *Poetics* is known to be one of the least well-preserved texts from classical Greece.

We also know that Aristotle wrote other works on literary subjects that have gone missing. Contemporary sources mention the three books of *On Poets*, written as dialogues, and *Homeric Problems*, in six or more books. We do have fragments from the first of these, but they are, indeed, so fragmentary as to be close to useless. A knowledge of these texts is probably taken for granted in the *Poetics*, and this gives rise to further problems of understanding it. The *Poetics* is divided into two parts: the part we have deals with tragedy and epic, and the missing one deals with comedy and other subjects. The Italian philosopher Umberto Eco wrote a best-selling novel about this missing part of the *Poetics*, *The Name of the Rose*.[17] We do not have to try to guess the contents of this part in order to busy our minds. The *Poetics*, as we have seen, is difficult enough in the parts that we do have present.

So what does Aristotle answer to the charges brought by Plato's Socrates? In short, Socrates argues in *Ion* that literature is not a skill, a *techne*, but only a matter of inspiration and possession. Against this Aristotle shows that literature is indeed a skill, and the *Poetics* is a discussion of 'the tools of the trade'. Aristotle was probably the first to use rational means to analyse what made good literature good. Plato further argues in the *Republic* that literature fires the passions to such an extent that reason and rationality are bypassed, and the whole fabric of society is at risk. This is one reason why the poets and rhapsodes are to be banned from the ideal republic. Aristotle agrees that literature works through the emotions, but thinks that this might be a good thing. We shall examine this view below, when we first acquire a background in his ethics, and then try to understand the central concept of *catharsis*.

Plato also held that the world we can sense is only a pale copy of an altogether more perfect and ideal reality beyond what we can sense. Since literature, and the other arts, only copy the world we can sense, art and literature takes us further away from ideal reality, and into illusion and falsehood. Again, Aristotle agrees that literature is a representation of reality, or the reality we can sense, but holds that this kind of representation is useful, and that we can learn from it.

The crucial concept here is *mimesis*,[18] translated as 'imitation' or 'representation'. This concept is widely discussed, not least with reference to Aristotle and Plato.[19] A possible way to discover the difference between Plato and Aristotle on the question of the relationship between literature and reality is that Aristotle famously claims that 'the difference is that [history] relates things that have happened, [literature] things that may happen. For this reason poetry is a more philosophical and more serious thing than history; poetry tends to speak of universals, history of particulars' (*Poetics*, 51b4–8).

Plato, on the other hand, seems to hold that literature just imitates, a mindless action, and moreover that literature finds it so much easier to imitate what is bad, than what is good.

'The other part of us, which remembers our sufferings and is never tired of bemoaning them, we may, I think, call irrational and lazy and inclined to cowardice.'

'Yes, we may.'

'And this recalcitrant element in us gives plenty of material for dramatic representation; but the reasonable element and its unvarying calm are difficult to represent. . . . The dramatic poet . . . will find it easy to represent a character that is unstable and refractory.'

(*The Republic*, 604d–605a)

The dangerous bit is that 'the dramatic poet produces a similar state of affairs in the mind of the individual, by encouraging the unreasoning part of it' (*The Republic*, 605b). Aristotle holds that the *mimesis* of literature is a representation of essences and universals, not of particulars and trivialities. Literature misses out on details, but that affords a greater concentration on what is crucial, the essence of what is being represented. Representation, or *mimesis*, is not a case of copying, but a process requiring mental effort. The *mimesis* of literature, therefore, is not a second-rate activity with a potential for subverting the rational order, but a process which accentuates the true nature of what is represented, and therefore closer to philosophy even than history.

All in all, it may be that Plato's strongest charge against literature is that it encourages the emotions, and that good sense and reason therefore is pushed aside. It is probable that Aristotle wanted to counter this charge through the notion of *catharsis*. Given the difficulties of Aristotle's text, however, we will need support from the rest of his philosophy to make sense of this term. Aristotle wrote on nearly all imaginable topics, from animals, the gods, sporting heroes, and, of course, philosophy, and the importance and range of the latter is nearly impossible to overstate, so here we will have to concentrate on those parts of it most relevant to his *Poetics*, and that will have to be his ethics.

Again, his writings on ethics[20] are also notes for use in his Lyceum where Aristotle taught young aristocratic men. Given this public, a crucial question would be 'how to make your life happy?'. The Greek term is *eudaimonia*, which has been translated in a number of different ways, quite often as 'happiness'. *Eudaimonia* is sought for its own sake, and not as a means to another end. It may be more accurate to say 'successful', or 'flourishing', since the goal is less a state of bliss, than a process of activities to fulfil one's potentials. Anyway, how do we achieve *eudaimonia*? The highest kind of life is the one devoted to truth, to intellectual contemplation, *theoria*. We should use those abilities which make us human. Aristotle is quite clear that it is the rational life which is worth living, but to achieve something by means of one's abilities is more important than just to have those abilities. To pursue this kind of life clearly has no goals beyond itself, and is therefore particularly pure. But *theoria* is not the only kind of knowledge. *Techne* is the practical skill of, for instance, making things. The skill of making shoes is one example of a *techne*, but the aristocratic Aristotle does not value this kind of knowledge very highly.

That is not the case with *phronesis*, which we may translate as 'practical wisdom' or 'practical knowledge'. This kind of knowledge applies to the social world, the world which is governed and shaped by human action. The laws of nature do not apply here, and *phronesis* is unlike *theoria* in being action-directed. It relates to the role of wisdom in guiding your actions, and in the exercise of *phronesis* you draw on your knowledge both of what is best for us on the highest level, and your knowledge and appraisal of the specific situation you are in. Only if you apply the relevant aspects of what is right to do generally can you have any hope of acting virtuously. You must, therefore, draw on your general knowledge of what is the right thing to do, but also draw on previous experience and your full knowledge of the people you deal with and the situation which both they and you are in. No easy matter, of course, and highly reliant on previous experience.

This is quite unlike Plato's views, or rather what we may assume could have been Plato's views. In the *Republic* every matter of its organisation is ultimately derived from the cosmic order, the real world beyond of which we can have sense-impressions. The ultimate reality is the guide for us, both in organising the political system and in our actions. It is by imitating the order of the realm of the forms that we can achieve the good life. Not so for Aristotle. He distinguishes between different realms of human life, and the methodology both of investigating these realms, and in implementing our knowledge is different. In the social realm we cannot apply strict laws that have no exceptions. To act in the best possible way toward a person, Karen, you have to use everything you know about her, her reactions and her goals in life (just to mention a few factors). This may be quite different to how you act towards Peter, even if the other factors in the situation are similar – just because Peter is likely to react differently because of the kind of person you take him to be.

So, *phronesis* is indeed wisdom. Acting and behaving in daily life is no easy matter, and definitely not a matter of applying strict laws. It is the skill of juggling all kinds of considerations with a view to acting – and swiftly – that is *phronesis*. This skill includes both means and objectives, as well as a keen perception of what kind of situation you are in. There is no time to sit down and think deeply about what is at hand, you need to act there and then. This is one reason why Aristotle puts such a great emphasis on developing habits. Learning to act correctly, and preferably with the right emotions to match, is very important. In developing habits, the actions we actually do perform are the building blocks. We become what we do, in a way.

Aristotle holds that passions and emotions are educable, and 'doing the right thing' teaches you to match actions and emotions. By doing what is right, the person's character is formed such that it will be drawn towards the appropriate or suitable things in life. But what is 'the right thing' for Aristotle, how does he define virtue? Obviously, this varies. However, generally speaking, it is right to avoid the extremes and keep to the mean. Do not act like a coward, and neither should you act foolishly. Aristotle is famous for his doctrine of 'the mean'. This 'mean' need not be directly in the middle, figuratively speaking of course, of any possible course of action. In the case of being foolhardy and a coward, the 'mean' action, being brave, is 'much closer' to the foolhardy than to the cowardly.

But how do the emotions fit into this? I have remarked earlier that you should also feel appropriately in doing the action. Is not this asking too much? Not according to Aristotle. In being generous and therefore acting virtuously, and avoiding the extremes of being stingy or extravagant, you also have to feel generous. If you give of yourself and your money in appropriate amounts, but feel terrible about it – that you begrudge the recipient every penny or every step you carry the load – then you are not generous. You are not generous if you act generously, but really hate it. It is because the emotions are rational and can be taught that they can be evaluated in this way, and you really can be taught to be generous – but only through learning to act and feel in unison. To go back to what we started with, the successful life, living well, *eudaimonia*, can not be obtained when you are in great inner tension between how you act and what you feel. *Eudaimonia*, and acting virtuously through the use of your *phronesis*, involves your whole personality and, therefore, also the emotions.

It is important, however, that the irrational elements of your soul are under the control of the rational ones. Philosophers, because of their profession, perhaps, tend to emphasise the rational element of our minds. Aristotle, however, emphasises habit and the importance of a set personality. Some reasons for this are that since emotions are not always controllable, and in some cases completely uncontrollable, they have to be moulded and formed through habitation, governed by the *ethos* and the laws of society, through the wisdom of the elders. We shall see in Chapter 7 that this view is held by some even in current debates about the role of literature in moral education and philosophy.

This short and compressed presentation of Aristotle's ethics should help us to understand the concept '*catharsis*' in the *Poetics*, which may be the main element in Aristotle's answer to the charges brought against literature by Plato. Let us first have a look at what Aristotle says about *catharsis*, and this is all he says about it in the *Poetics*, in his definition of tragedy:

> Tragedy is a representation of a serious, complete action which has magnitude, in embellished speech, with each of its elements used separately in the various parts of the play; represented by people acting and not by narration; accomplishing by means of pity and terror the *catharsis* of such emotions.
>
> (*Poetics*, 49b25–28)

The starting point of the whole phenomenon of tragedies, apparently, was the ritual performed in the honour of the god Dionysus. It was an annual purgation or purification of the poisons which had contaminated society with sin and with death in the year past, and the term '*catharsis*' itself has most often been translated as 'purification' or 'cleansing'. It is worth keeping in mind that in the year 361 BC, in Aristotle's own time, tragedies were introduced in Rome. This did not happen for artistic reasons, but for superstitious ones. They were used as a *catharmos*, a cleaning out, of pestilence. It is therefore possible that Aristotle uses these models, but gives them a new meaning – a meaning clear and obvious to the students and participants in his Lyceum, but hard to uncover for us. It is also interesting to note that some of the phenomena about which Aristotle actually used *catharsis* in his biological writings were menstruation, birth and the ejaculation of semen. Again, the best we can do is to go through the written evidence in the *Poetics* and try to construct the best possible understanding of the text.

As mentioned already, the most widely accepted interpretation is that Aristotle meant that a *catharsis* was a 'cleaning out' of feelings. This view came to prominence with an essay by Jacob Bernays in 1857.[21] The only 'evidence' we have for such a reading is a passage in *The Politics*, book VIII.7. (1341–2). He does not explain here what he means by the term, but rather unhelpfully refers to a fuller treatment in his *Poetics*. This must mean that the passage has not survived, or that it was never written. Anyway, what he says about *cathartic* songs in *The Politics* is that they arouse the emotions of people suffering from hysterical emotions, and thus relieve them. However, an audience for a tragedy would not be composed of people who are insane or otherwise in need of emotional purgation for reasons of poor mental health. An audience would presumably also include virtuous persons, and these are not pathological cases.

This means that *catharsis* cannot be a purification in a literal sense, since the typical audience at the theatre is not poisoned or collectively sick for other reasons. And if we look more closely at what Aristotle thought of the emotions, there is quite a lot that indicates that he did not see them as phenomena that were easily purged. Fear, for example, he sees as a 'pain or agitation derived from the imagination of a future destructive or painful evil'.[22] Fear is thus not only the sensation, it also requires the belief that one is in danger. You have, in other words, to be in a state of mind where the danger is worthy of fear. You are not in fear if you think for sure you will be able to avoid the danger. When you drive down a road at fifty miles an hour and meet cars coming in the opposite direction, you do not feel fear – and that is because you believe they will keep to the other lane. Similarly in the theatre: sitting on the back row you do not think you are about to die from the sword drawn by the actor against the protagonist.

A further explanation for our understanding of this term, is that *catharsis* provides an education or clarification of the emotions.[23] This view has a lot to recommend it. We saw when going through Aristotle's views on ethics that he wanted education to comprise of getting youths to feel pleasure and pain for the right things; to take pleasure in acting justly, and to feel pain with the opposite. In order to build a settled character you also have to have the right feelings given the situation you are in, it is no use trying to reason with powerful emotions. Therefore, if tragedy can educate us to feel appropriately outside the fictional setting of the theatre, it would find its place in an ethical education. This view also provides an account of the particular pleasures we have in the performance of a tragedy. Aristotle also argued that there is an in-built desire in human beings to understand, and that there is a particular pleasure in having it satisfied. Seen in this way, tragedy provides a particular cognitive pleasure in that we become more able to understand the human condition, and also to adjust the full range of our being, both the cognitive faculties as well as our emotions.

It would be nice if this could be the last word about the understanding of the term *catharsis*, but it also comes up short on some points. A virtuous person attending the performance of a tragedy will also experience a *catharsis*, as Aristotle makes clear in the last part of the *Poetics* when he talks about the cultivated audience. Aristotle has two clearly defined kinds of audience, one educated and one consisting of the 'ordinary' people. In both cases they are already formed, so any ethical education will come too late. It is therefore hard to escape the conclusion that for Aristotle education is something for children and the young, and tragical *catharsis* is something for grown-ups, even virtuous persons who do not, by definition, need any education in these matters.

There are further reasons why *catharsis* as education cannot be the last word on the matter. If tragedy is to be an educational experience, then the emotions we feel in the theatre should be the same as we would feel in real life. But this is fortunately not the case. In real life it would be completely bizarre to take pleasure in events presented in a tragedy. First of all, we should not be trained to seek out tragedy in real life, as we do in the theatre, and second we should not be trained to find pleasure in real tragic events. After all, it is just because a representation is a representation, and not real life, that a kind of pleasure is a suitable response to it. The tragedian should call forth fear and pity through a *mimesis* of such events, as we have seen in the crucial quotation in the *Poetics*. It is in the *catharsis* of such emotions that literature goes beyond what is suitable as reactions to such events in real life. Neither the understanding of *catharsis* as purgation nor as education of the emotions are sufficient because they do not explain the particular pleasures attendant on tragedy as literary composition.

Are these pleasures bound to pity and fear? In a way they are, but pity and fear are causally prior to *catharsis* in that they are not the proper effect of tragedy, and neither is the cognitive pleasure of following the plot, even if it is only through following the plot that we can be filled with pity and fear. These emotions are important, but Aristotle says that it is *by means of pity and fear* that tragedy creates a *catharsis* of these emotions. This amounts to a non-cognitive view of *catharsis* and the pleasures of tragedy, in that it denies that the pleasures of tragedy can be *identified* with cognitive (or learning-related) pleasures.

That the proper tragic pleasures are pity and fear is stated clearly in the *Poetics*, and they are, moreover, produced by the representation of a particular kind of terrible incident, *pathos*. The kind of terrible incidents referred to are those between relations or lovers, and what is particularly terrible about these is that they can happen to anyone. For the bringing forth of fear it is required that the incident is conceivable as a painful and destructive incident which could happen to you, and as far as pity is concerned, the terrible incidents others are subjected to can happen to us and to those who are closest to us. Their situation, therefore, has to be quite similar to our own. However, it being able to happen to us and those closest to us must not be too threatening or imminent, or fear would drive pity out. A normal member of the audience, therefore, must be able to think that what happens on stage can happen to him or her. Without this, the member of the audience would not be able to feel the tragic feelings.

Could this happen on the basis of empathy? No, we must be sufficiently similar to those characters on stage, but not feel immediate empathy. The tragic heroes such as Oedipus, or even Hamlet, are both like and unlike ourselves. Sufficiently similar to ourselves for us to feel pity, but different enough to avoid empathy. Normal members of the audience attending a tragedy believe that the terrible events being presented could, possibly, happen to them, no matter that it is not very likely statistically that your uncle murders your father and marries your mother as in *Hamlet*. Given this, then there are some facts that characterise this typical member of the audience both before and after the play: he or she does have those emotions and beliefs ('it could happen to me') that would characterise fear and pity. In other words: normal and educated people have beliefs that they do not feel. The pleasure experienced depends in great measure on the awareness that this is only a representation, a *mimesis*, and that it is just this *mimesis* you react to. In the theatre we can, in an imaginary setting, take full emotional account of something we reckon to be but a distant possibility. The tragedian wakes us to the fact that there are some emotional possibilities that we overlook in real life. On the other hand, this allows us to step out of everyday drudgery for the duration of the play, and opens up the possibility that our lives can be torn apart, while all the time we know that we do not have to meet the full consequences.

It is probably this experience of the tragical emotions in a place nothing like real life, the theatre, that explains our feeling relief. The relief is not the liberation of the bottled up emotions *as such*, but the relief in giving vent to them in safety. However, to say that this was the feeling of 'release' that Aristotle called *catharsis* is not a sufficient characteristic: one also needs to know what our release is *about*. Aristotle knew and showed that the tragical world has to be rational. The events in tragedy have to happen because of other events, and the consequences of the original events have to be probable. A good tragedy thus gives us some consolation, in that even when the most basic lines in life are cut, it does not happen in a chaotic and meaningless universe. There is also a consolation in knowing that things cannot get any worse, and that the world is still a rational and meaningful place.[24]

FURTHER READING

Plato on literature: G. R. F. Ferrari, 'Plato and Poetry', in *The Cambridge History of Literary Criticism: Volume 1 – Classical Criticism*, ed. by George A. Kennedy (Cambridge: Cambridge University Press, 1989), pp. 92–148).

Plato in general: a collection of essays both on his background and some themes from his philosophy is *The Cambridge Companion to Plato*, ed. Richard Kraut (Cambridge: Cambridge University Press, 1992).

Aristotle's *Poetics*: this has given rise to a number of commentaries over the years. One of the most recent is Stephen Halliwell, 'Aristotle's Poetics', in *The Cambridge History of Literary Criticism: Volume 1 – Classical Criticism*, edited by George A. Kennedy (Cambridge: Cambridge University Press, 1989), pp. 149–83. A recent collection of essays is *Essays on Aristotle's Poetics*, edited by Amélie Oksenberg Rorty (Princeton, NJ: Princeton University Press, 1992).

Aristotle in general: A collection of essays on central themes of his philosophy is *The Cambridge Companion to Aristotle*, ed. Jonathan Barnes (Cambridge: Cambridge University Press, 1995). The bibliography takes up no less than 84 pages, which goes to show that there is no shortage of material on Aristotle.

Both Plato and Aristotle: Eva Schaper, *Prelude to Aesthetics* (London: Allen and Unwin, 1968) traces the earliest philosophical treatment of problems relating to literature and the arts in Plato and Aristotle, and particularly how these areas relate to other areas of human concern.

NOTES

1. Alberto Manguel, *A History of Reading* (London: Flamingo, 1997), 'The Silent Readers', pp. 41–54.
2. Plato, *The Republic*, book X, 607b. Quotations and references to the *Republic* are from the translation by Desmond Lee, second edn (Harmondsworth: Penguin, 1974).
3. An introduction to Plato's views on literature can be found in G. R. F. Ferrari, 'Plato and Poetry', in George A. Kennedy (ed.), *The Cambridge History of Literary Criticism: Volume 1 – Classical Criticism* (Cambridge: Cambridge University Press, 1989), pp. 92–148.
4. This has been argued by, among others, Dalia Judovitz in 'Philosophy and Poetry: The Difference Between Them in Plato and Descartes', in Anthony J. Cascardi (ed.), *Literature and the Question of Philosophy* (Baltimore, MD: Johns Hopkins University Press, 1987), pp. 26–51 (p. 27).
5. Readers should keep this in mind, since I shall refer to Plato's philosophy and beliefs without having anything but the views expressed by characters in his dialogues as evidence.
6. Thomas A. Szlezák, *Reading Plato*, trans. Graham Zanker (London: Routledge, 1999), argues this view.
7. Plato, *Ion*, trans. Lane Cooper, in Edith Hamilton and Huntingdon Cairns (eds), *The Collected Works of Plato: Including the Letters*, Bollingen Series 71 (Princeton, NJ: Princeton University Press, 1989), pp. 215–28.

8. Plato, *Protagoras* (325e–326a), trans. W. K. C. Guthrie, in Edith Hamilton and Huntington Cairns (eds), *The Collected Works of Plato: Including the Letters*, pp. 308–52.
9. A philosopher is literally a lover of wisdom. *Sophos* is wisdom in Greek, and the root *philo* denotes love, but not erotic desire, for which the root is *eros* (as in the modern 'erotic'). See Plato's dialogue *Phaedrus*, 278d, where he introduces the term 'philosopher'.
10. See also Penelope Murray, 'Inspiration and *Mimesis* in Plato', in Andrew Barker and Martin Warner (eds), *The Language of the Cave* (Edmonton, Alberta: Academic Printing and Publishing, 1992), pp. 27–46 (p. 28).
11. I have learnt from Alexander Nehamas, 'Plato and the Mass Media', *The Monist*, 71 (1988), pp. 214–34.
12. To borrow a phrase from Wayne C. Booth, a book of his is called *The Company We Keep: An Ethics of Fiction* (Berkeley, CA: University of California Press, 1988).
13. Aristotle, *The Politics*, trans. T. A. Sinclair, revised edn (London: Penguin, 1992), VII, 1336b.
14. Wayne C. Booth, 'The Company We Keep: Self-Making in Imaginative Art', *Daedalus*, 111 (1982), 56–7. Quoted by Nehamas, 'Plato and the Mass Media', p. 221.
15. Arthur Picard-Cambridge, *The Theatre of Dionysus in Athens* (Oxford: Clarendon Press, 1946), and *The Dramatic Festivals of Athens*, 2nd edn (Oxford: Clarendon Press, 1968), and Peter Walcot, *Greek Drama in its Theatrical and Social Context* (Cardiff: University of Wales Press, 1976).
16. *The Poetics* has been translated into a number of different languages, and in a wide variety of editions. I have used *Poetics: With the 'Tractatus Coislinianus', Reconstruction of 'Poetics II', and the Fragments of 'On Poets'*, trans. Richard Janko (Indianapolis, IN: Hackett, 1987). This edition has a useful introduction and copious notes.
17. Umberto Eco, *The Name of the Rose*, trans. W. Weaver (London: Secker & Warburg, 1983). Some will know the film better, with Sean Connery in the leading role.
18. The Swedish scholar Göran Sörbom's *Mimesis and Art: Studies in the Origin and Early Development of an Aesthetic Vocabulary* (Stockholm: Bonnier, 1966) is a seminal work on the etymology and philosophical importance of this concept.
19. A standard work on *mimesis* in western literature is Erich Auerbach's *Mimesis: The Representation of Reality in Western Literature*, trans. Willard R. Trask (Princeton, NJ: Princeton University Press, 1953).
20. The main source is the *Nicomachean Ethics*, trans. Terence Irwin (Indianapolis, IN: Hackett, 1987).
21. Jacob Bernays, *Grundzüge der verlorenen Abhandlung des Aristoteles über Wirkung der Tragödie* (Breslau, 1857). My source is Richard Janko's introduction to Aristotle's *Poetics*, pp. xvi–xvii.

22. Aristotle, *On Rhetoric: A Theory of Civic Discourse*, trans. George A. Kennedy (New York: Oxford University Press, 1991), II, 5, 1382a.

23. This is a view put forward by, among others, Martha Nussbaum, see her book *The Fragility of Goodness: Luck and Ethics in Greek Tragedy and Philosophy* (Cambridge: Cambridge University Press, 1986).

24. The view presented here owes a debt to Jonathan Lear's '*Katharsis*', in Amélie Oksenberg Rorty (ed.), *Essays on Aristotle's Poetics* (Princeton, NJ: Princeton University Press, 1992), pp. 315–40.

THREE

DEFINING LITERATURE

We have just seen how Aristotle defined Tragedy, and he did so through the enjoyment or pleasure particular to Tragedy. For him, the value of tragedy was intimately connected with the way in which it was defined. In a way, he could have said that if Tragedy does not create fear and pity, and a *catharsis* of these emotions, it is not a tragedy. It should be clear, therefore, that Aristotle in this way introduced a *stipulative* definition of tragedy since not everything that is performed as a tragedy can pass muster and become tragedy. But what of literature as a whole, and literature as we know the phenomenon today – can and should this be defined?

Any definition must have a purpose, and we should not be content to say that since philosophy is in the business of defining things, literature should also be defined. In the previous chapter we saw that Plato tried to discredit literature since it was in competition with the role he assigned to philosophy. The place of literature in the lives of people today, and as an 'institution' in the fabric of modern society, makes literature a different phenomenon from that which Plato and Aristotle disagreed about. In this chapter, therefore, I shall start with the reasons we may have for wanting to define literature, and then discuss ways of defining, not only literature, but other phenomena as well, before presenting and analysing different suggested definitions. This process will also reveal something about the nature of philosophy, but this will not be the main theme of the chapter.

WHY DEFINE LITERATURE?

Yes, what is the point?[1] A perfectly reasonable response may be that we know full well what literature is, and that this business of always having to define this, that and the other is just an intellectualistic prejudice best left on the scrap-heap. After all, the world is a diverse and varied place, and the habit of forcing all cultural phenomena into strictly defined categories carries the danger of radically reducing them. The upshot of such wanton defining, in turn, is that we are left with a limited understanding of it, and something much poorer than the rich variety of life. Given the existence of this chapter and its length it must be clear that I do not share the latter view, though I do share some of the misgivings about going hell-for-leather into the definition business. This is why we need to look more closely at the reasons for wanting to define it. One answer to 'why define literature?' is that it is no longer evident that literature is worth studying. When the ideals of *bildung*, a character-forming education, were beyond question the value and importance of literature was also not questioned. You were to study the best of what was said and written in western culture, the whole canon from Homer, or even *Gilgamesh*, to maybe Kafka or whatever author was the latest to be admitted to the canon. The nature and importance of literature was given by tradition and the criteria laid down by the exemplary writers.

This view is no longer unchallenged. First of all, it is no longer, if it ever was, *comme il faut* to take tradition on trust. From Marx, Nietzsche and Freud came currents of thinking that have been referred to as 'the hermeneutics of suspicion'. The tradition was seen variously as the product of dominant classes wanting to suppress the masses, corrupt, or as the symptom of repressed desire. With feminism came an added element to this; the fact that women have been neglected in literary history, and that the canon is dominated by men. This means, of course, that the male perspective dominates throughout the history of literary production and reading. The tradition is no longer universally accepted and trusted as the product of 'the test of time',[2] through which only the best works survive, but a product of the male domination in western culture. We have an acronym to describe this phenomenon: DWEM (Dead White European Males). Our western culture and literature has been created and defined by this category of person, and their views are therefore dominant, not only in our culture, but because of cultural imperialism also in non-western cultures. This cultural domination marginalises living black African women, to pick but one obvious example. The works and authors that have been held up as perhaps even defining the humane qualities of a civilised society, such as Homer, Sophocles, Dante, Shakespeare, Goethe and others, have really only been representative of the male ruling classes. Their views and outlook is not that of humanity as such, but of the interests and preoccupations of a numerically very minor part of humanity, and one that has an interest in maintaining the *status quo*.

Does this 'charge' (note how adversarial the metaphors of argument are) really kill the idea or concept of literature? There is obviously a great deal to recommend the view just presented, but it also needs to be nuanced a little. Not only were the names in the canon DWEMs, they were also literate DWEMs. Apart from China, only the European/ Middle-Eastern cultures were literate ones up until fairly recently, historically speaking. Only men had a position in these societies which made writing possible. However, the weakest link in the DWEM argumentation is that it claims that DWEM literary culture is monolithic. The contrary is the case. Over the two or three millennia it covers, great changes have been seen. Literary culture originated in the near east, in societies very different even from medieval Europe. A whole plethora of views and attitudes are reflected in this tradition, though they are certainly predominantly written by men. In this, literary history is a reflection of relations of power in society, but these relations have also changed over time. Until a few hundred years ago, though, almost only men were in power. So, the charges of the DWEM variety are true in general, but what action, if any, should we take on this? Should we suppress works of fiction written at a time with an outlook other than our own? Do we know for sure that our own views and attitudes are the best and final in history? Are we on the last rung of a ladder leading up to the ultimate ethical position? Most of us would like that to be the case, of course, but confronting views other than our own, particularly when we are likely to dislike them, may be valuable in itself since it makes us realise that beliefs and views we regard as preposterous were foundations of the world view of other times and cultures. If nothing else, this can make us see that our own beliefs are just beliefs, and not one of the facts of human existence. One may argue that people in general, and students in particular, are not really such tender plants that they should not read literature reflecting views different from those deemed correct in the present day.

This is one possible line of argument to defend the tradition and the concept of literature, despite the relevant arguments about the views reflected in older works. For our purposes, the DWEM argument is one reason why the authority of the tradition can no longer be invoked to justify the value of literature. This leaves a vacuum where the values inherent in literature, if any, require a defence. This is also made evident by various versions of post-modernism which claim that the category of literature cannot be said to exist in any coherent form, and that what are called works of literature are just texts like other texts. Many of these views are to be found in 'readers' and textbooks on 'literary theory', but the purpose of defining literature must also be to find out what literary theory is a theory *of*. To see literature as just text requires that one conveniently forgets that they are created by human beings who are, by nature, social animals who, at least sometimes, do things with a purpose and expect others to recognise that purpose. We do not just create strings of symbols for no reason at all, but we wish these strings to fulfil functions which may differ from one kind of text to another. To most people the phonebook is not a good read, but it can be quite useful if you want to know somebody's phone number. The newspaper may be a good source for the news, but what the purpose is of works marketed as literature is not so obvious.

Some people think that literature is just a convenient topic for chit-chat, and a good number of theorists of literature have, perhaps unwittingly, spent a lot of time producing arguments that can be taken to support this view. My point is that the need to clarify literature as a field of value is also a political undertaking – it is the defence of a cultural institution. This is the anti-philistine reason why literature is worth defining. In many countries the production of literature, as well as its dissemination, is subsidised by the public purses, and literature has to defend its place in direct competition with spending on such things as health, infrastructure and defence. If we can define literature so as to clarify an important cultural institution, then we shall also have conducted a work of political importance. Defining literature, therefore, is part of a defence of its claim to our time and attention, but this in its turn requires something about the nature and quality of the definition. This preamble has not taken us any nearer such a definition, but we have, at least, laid down some guidelines as to how the result must be in order to serve the purpose.

My aim here is not to arrive at my own ultimate definition of literature, but there are already several others in the field worth discussing. However, we shall have to look into the nature of definitions and their role in philosophy before we go into the specific definitions of literature.

HOW TO DEFINE LITERATURE

In Chapter 2 we saw that Plato wanted to establish philosophy as the only reliable way to truth, and that a vital part of his strategy was to discredit the rivals – including literature. His is also the first known use of the word 'methodos' ('method'), but what is the method of philosophy? How does philosophy gain insight into the various aspects of the world? Plato can be read as proposing a complete philosophy in the middle dialogues, where the main feature is the theory of 'forms', also known as 'ideas'. These are immutable constituents of ultimate reality, and the world we perceive around us is only a pale and imperfect reflection of this remote realm.

How can we gain insight into the forms? Well, Plato scholars are not always in agreement on this, but since our business here is not to establish the final view on Plato but to get a clearer idea about definitions, we should instead look at an early dialogue where he uses the method of *elenchus* to clarify or define central concepts. This involves question and answer, and usually two people for the roles. The questioner, usually a character called Socrates who shares most of the traits we know the historical Socrates to have possessed, asks some portentous question such as 'what is justice?', 'what is courage?' – or as in our example below: 'what is beauty?'. The answerer is usually someone who should be in a position to know the answer. Then several answers are tried and found wanting by the questioner, usually because they turn out to be inconsistent with other things the answerer believes. The result is always that we do not know, we are left, it seems, where we began.

But if Plato was such a great philosopher, why did he not figure out the truth and then preach the truth from some mountain, or have them inscribed on stone tablets? Plato's protagonist, Socrates, goes instead to great lengths to establish his deep ignorance. In the dialogue *Meno* he says that 'it is not from any sureness in myself that I cause others to doubt; it is from being more in doubt than anyone else that I cause doubt in others' (80c). But then what is the use? The discussion shows that people use the same words, but that they either mean different things with them, or even mean nothing at all. The process brings them closer to at least talking about the same thing.

Let us see how this dialogue by Plato – or perhaps we should say a 'platonic dialogue' because it is not certain that *Hippias Major*[3] is by Plato – shows the use of the *elenchus*. It could also have been written by a pupil of Plato in the Academy as an exercise, but we cannot be sure. The topic for discussion, in any case, is 'beauty', and Socrates meets Hippias, a rich and famous sophist, and after a long preamble about the exploits of Hippias they enter into a discussion about *kalon*, 'the beautiful' or 'the fine' (as it has also been translated). Socrates is cunning in using a fictitious character who supposedly once asked Socrates about what beauty was, since this feature allows him to manipulate and even make fun of Hippias without being directly to blame (but it seems that Hippias smells a rat anyway).

In summary, their discussion goes like this: Socrates proposes that all beautiful things are beautiful by beauty, and not by anything else (287c9), and this is the guide for the whole discussion. There cannot be something not beautiful which makes it thus. Hippias proposes a series of things or situations that are beautiful, but Socrates remains unimpressed. He keeps coming back to the question of what qualities there are in the beautiful that makes it beautiful, what makes it beautiful by its beauty. Hippias proposes that a beautiful girl is beautiful, and that gold makes things beautiful. He even says that burying your parents is a beautiful thing to do, but Socrates is no nearer the beauty of the beautiful. These are all beautiful things, examples, but not 'the real thing'. Then comes a series of suggestions from Socrates' questioner which may be more fruitful, but even these turn out not to be satisfactory. The dialogue ends by Socrates concluding that 'the proverb says "all that is beautiful is difficult" – I think I know *that*' (304e9). Socratic dialogues characteristically end in an *aporia*, literally a dead end, from which you do not know where to go next.

But is that all we have learnt? This dialogue has been read as an early one, and it probably is, if it is written by Plato at all, but it points forward to the theory of the forms in that it is the nature and quality of beauty in itself that is being sought. Plato, in the middle dialogues at least, operates at an ontological level, the level of true being in itself. He was not interested in discovering how we use words, but to define the truly existing form of beauty. We have at least seen where not to turn for an answer, and we must also remember that the kind of questioning Socrates represents was new to the time. These days we are quite used to questions about the essence of things, even pop songs ask about 'the meaning of love'. But to Plato's time and world this was new. So what is the essence of *kalon*, the fine or beautiful? We do not know, but we do know that for any suggestion to qualify it will have to be what makes all *kalon* things *kalon*, and for this to be true *kalon* will have to be the same in all its instances. It will have to be of a particular nature, and it is precisely this nature which is sought.

Will this have to be the case when we search for a definition of literature, too? We still operate with mostly the same picture of defining and definitions that we got from Plato and Aristotle, but with the important proviso that they wanted 'real definitions', definitions of things and not of words.[4] When Socrates in *Hippias Major* asks 'what is beauty?' he does not want to know how one is to use the word, but to clarify the really existing thing beauty. When we today want to characterise and 'nail down' a phenomenon we try to define necessary and sufficient criteria of what it is, we define words through the use of other words. The technical terms we use are *definiens* and *definiendum*. The latter is what is to be defined, such as 'literature', and the former is what defines it, and to discuss different suggestions as to what is to be the *definiens* of 'literature' is the main business of this chapter.

Definitions can be of different kinds, and the main ones today are 'descriptive' and 'stipulative'. The former keeps to what is the reigning understanding of the term or concept, and is the kind you may find in dictionaries. Stipulative definitions are also called 'normative', and may say how the term should be understood – either for a specific use in the text to follow, or it may have wider ambitions in wanting to substitute the settled norm with a better understanding of the term or concept in question. In the case of 'literature' we have a fairly wide definition which you may find in dictionaries, such that the *definiens* of 'literature' is 'all the writings of a country'. This was about the only definition of the term up until about two centuries ago. Literature included not only works of fiction, but also historical, religious and scientific writings. The change to a more restricted understanding of 'literature', to comprise mainly fictional works with artistic pretensions, the *belles-lettres*, was very gradual and may not even be complete today – as the dictionary versions attest.

We may imagine Socrates discussing the definition of literature with Ion, for instance. It is a fair guess that he would not be content with the dictionary's definition, but would be searching for the 'essence', the 'literariness of literature'. Present-day sociologists, on the other hand, may not be similarly concerned; they would see literature as a social phenomenon and would perhaps treat the desire to identify the true nature and essence of literature with derision. It is also likely that they would be searching for easily identifiable traits that could be used in a survey of literature. The end determines the means, and in the social sciences the definition of a phenomenon should both capture the present use of the term, and be easy to operationalise in a survey. This is not the way we want to approach the phenomenon of literature here, but one remark may be in order. On the back cover of paperbacks you often see some text immediately above the recommended retail price, or somewhere on the lower part of the page. On some books you will see 'fiction', on others 'literature' (as well as 'history', 'reference', 'biography' and all the rest, of course). 'Literature' is usually reserved for the more 'worthy' books, and goes to show that the term is used evaluatively. It is not just a category like any other, but is used to signify that the book is more valuable than mere 'fiction'. Any story which is not presented as true can be fiction, but not all of the latter are 'literature'. But what we want to know is how we can distinguish these works, and by virtue of which quality or set of qualities we can claim that they are better than the mere fictitious works.

WHAT LITERATURE IS

A part of this quest may involve just where the literariness of literature is said to reside. Is it something you can read off the page, something you can spot 'with the naked eye', or do you have to be especially equipped for the purpose? In aesthetics, the philosophy of art, the main question can be said to have moved from 'what is beauty?' to the more urgent 'what is art?'. The latter question may be urgent because it is so easily misled. When Duchamp put a urinal in an art gallery and called it a work of art, things changed. 'Art' certainly changed from being a fairly unproblematic category to being even the subject matter of many works of art (if that is what they were). The concept of 'found art' was also introduced, where objects literally picked off the ground were declared to be art, and either exhibited untouched where found, or brought to some gallery and put on exhibition.

How can this be explained? A common-sensical view of art is that artworks have particular qualities put there, somehow, by the artist. The qualities that made the work art was there to be seen, even if you needed some background and perhaps even education to be able to see them. With Immanuel Kant's so-called third critique, *The Critique of Judgement*,[5] the focus on the work itself changed, and turned over to the subject of the aesthetic experience. Kant, though not the first to do so,[6] insisted that the aesthetic attitude was of a particular kind, and completely disinterested. The nature of this attitude is what it is not: it is not practical, moral or self-interested, and any value we experience in it is therefore not related to anything else. Aesthetic values are therefore autonomous, they are not derivable from anything else, and this view in due course became the central tenet of different movements emphasising aesthetic autonomy: that the aesthetic realm is divorced from other aspects of experience.

We therefore have two different types of possible answer to the question of where the 'literariness' of literature can be found. We may call these 'externalist', for those who believe that the necessary and sufficient criteria can be found 'outside', in the work, and 'internalist' for those who believe that the criteria are to be found in the subject, or subjects, be they authors or readers. These types of definition are, however, only types. This distinction is not absolute, and few of the theorists themselves think of their own contributions as belonging to any of these two types. This division is a heuristic one, and whether or not it is fruitful can only be decided on the basis of the following explanations.

EXTERNALIST THEORIES

These definitions claim that all the criteria necessary and sufficient to judge a work to be a literary one are syntactic, semantic and/or structural features of the text itself, and you therefore need no knowledge about the writer's intentions or the reactions of the reader. All you need can be read directly off the page, so to speak. This view carries with it a number of implications which have to be looked at rather closely. For one thing, it implies that any aesthetic qualities and properties depend, in the last resort, on linguistic and rhetorical properties of the text itself, and that the aesthetic qualities can, ultimately, be reduced to the textual ones. To further investigate the claims of this group of theories we have to look more closely at specific theories. One of these is what we may call the semantic theory, closely associated with the American aesthetician Monroe C. Beardsley. Few people have been as influential in aesthetics in the twentieth century. Almost on his own, he brought aesthetics back into the mainstream of philosophy after decades of neglect with his book simply called *Aesthetics*.[7] In this book he also tries to define literature. Here is his, albeit tentative, definition: 'Tentatively, therefore, we may say that "literature" is well defined as "discourse with important implicit meaning".'[8]

What does this mean? It rests on a distinction between what a sentence means, and what it suggests, and supposes that where the difference between what we can call 'surface meaning' and 'real meaning' is particularly strong, we have a literary work. However, this is neither necessary nor sufficient. It is not necessary because there are works we would want to call literature which do not have this quality, or where the quality is nearly absent or unimportant. Consider the following passage from Doris Lessing's short story 'To Room Nineteen':

> Resentment. It was poisoning her. (She looked at this emotion and thought it was absurd. Yet she felt it.) She was a prisoner. (She looked at this thought too, and it was no good telling herself it was a ridiculous one.) She must tell Matthew – but what? She was filled with emotions that were utterly ridiculous, that she despised, yet that nevertheless she was feeling so strongly she could not shake them off.[9]

It is not obvious that there is a great deal of 'important implicit meaning' in this passage, and even if it were present to a large degree, it would not carry a label telling the reader of its function. Maybe it works better in the case of poetry, but even simple poems do not necessarily fit in.

Using 'semantic density' as a criterion would leave out a set of works which it would be counterintuitive to dismiss as literature. In cases where the terrain does not fit the map, we have to adjust the map. Leaving out vast chunks of what is considered literature would not be a discovery, it would just change the subject. We would end up talking about something other than literature, and that is why the semantic density criterion is not a necessary one.

Can it be sufficient, then? This would require that other kinds of discourse do not use 'semantic density'. This is not the case. There are several uses of language, even in writing, which also have important implicit meanings, such as jokes – or at least some kinds of jokes. Deadpan jokes can be funny just because of 'important implicit meanings'. Consider a rather bulky person who is run over by a car. The victim shouts to the driver: 'why couldn't you drive around me?', and the driver replies 'I didn't have enough petrol'. The important meaning, which makes the joke, is implicit. Does this, then, turn this exchange into literature? Hardly, and this is why it cannot be a sufficient criterion either.

Important implicit meanings do occur in literature, but not only in literature, and the crucial point is the use to which they are put. They are not normally laughed at, as with the jokes. The layers of meaning of a literary work are normally taken to have a function related to its status as literature. If you are in a situation where you have to communicate clearly and unambiguously, when you are helping the driver of a car to look out for traffic or writing an instruction manual for the use of explosives, important meanings that are only implicit are not only a pain, but can also be downright dangerous. For semantic density to work as a criterion you have to know *the purpose of the work*, since without this information it is impossible to understand *how* the semantic density works, and what it is *for*. Such a purpose is hard to read straight off the page, and this is precisely the chief weakness of these theories. We have to move away from the black marks on the page to determine whether some features are literary or not. Semantic density only has a function in a context, and such density cannot by itself make a page literary. Supporters would probably argue that semantic density fulfils an artistic function, but this is circular: to determine which discourses have this function is just to know what was to be defined: you know which works are literary. The logical steps are reversed.

The problems with the structuralist version of this kind of theory are the same. In the words of Roland Barthes: 'the structure of the sentence, the object of linguistics, is found again, homologically, in the structure of works. Discourse is not simply an adding together of sentences: it is, itself, one great sentence'.[10] Barthes later abandoned this view, but the point here is to illustrate this way of thinking about defining literature. It is trivial to say that there are structures in literary works. Of course there are, there are structures in almost anything you care to mention: even amoeba have structures. The point, however, is to find structures that are relevant. Literary works are not provided with a guide to their relevant features. These will have to be identified by the reader, and in order to do so the reader would have to be within a practice. Literature is not just any kind of text, there is a set of assumptions about how literature is to be approached in order to yield interesting readings. These are shared by writer, publisher and reader. To read Melville's *Moby Dick* as a plain tale of whaling is not to read it as literature, and the selection and interpretation of the relevant elements of the text to make it literature do not leap off the page to tell you who they are and what they are doing there.

Essential to the view of Barthes and others is the belief that literature is text. This implies that literature can be read and understood just like other forms of text, and then the relevance of linguistics and philosophical theories about the nature of language as such is pretty clear. One may find many interesting features and phenomena in this way, but it gives us no reason to value literature. Indeed, the very category of literature becomes meaningless. The view that literature is just text is also held by various deconstructive theories. A further discussion of both structuralism and deconstruction will have to be left for Chapter 4, when we are going to look at the implications of these theories for where we can locate the source of meaning in literary works.

We can learn something from the externalist type of theories, I think, and it is this: if you consider literature as text only it also ends up as a dead text-object where nothing of value can reside. If everything is text, then literature does not exist, and this is just a refusal to consider some texts as more valuable than others. Everything just turns into a grey mass. It is only if you see literature not only as text, but also as art, that you may be able to identify reasons why this class of texts is worth dealing with. If this is a part of the purpose of defining literature, then the externalist type of theory has little to offer.

INTERNALIST THEORIES

Now, if the source of 'the literary' cannot be found on the pages of the work, where can it reside? One answer could be that it is a matter of experience, or even a matter of intention. On the first criterion, if you experience that some work or other offers a valuable experience of a certain kind, then it is literature. On the second criterion, if you intend to make a literary work, then it is a literary work. Neither of these seem at first sight to be much better than the externalist theories. The externalist theories at least offered explanations of why certain works are counted as literary, and others not, and these had to do with observable traits in the works. It is not impossible that there must be something observable in the work at hand for us to count it as literature, and certainly that an act of will cannot suffice on its own.

Historically, the internalist tendency is linked to romanticism, with its emphasis on the particular gifts of the creative artist, and therefore had its heyday before externalist theories came on the scene. The latter was a reaction to the subjectivism of the internalist views – that something indefinable, such as the genius of the author, transformed a written narrative into great art worthy to be considered as literature. In modern versions the internalist view leaves the decision about whether the work is literature or not to the author. This has some obvious benefits in that it locates the responsibility somewhere, and it just remains for any reader to say whether the literary work is a good, bad or indifferent one. However, for the same reason it is also a cop-out: it just fails to define literature. It may be a more or less convenient way to decide in individual cases, but it says nothing about what kind of phenomenon literature is. If the President of the World Bank declared that his or her annual report is a work of literature, albeit a rather bad one, we would be no nearer an understanding of the phenomenon. But this is a bit like opening a Pandora's box. Internalist theories suffer from having no tools with which to divide intentions in works from those that occur in all other kinds of contexts, since these may also throw some light on what the author meant. If somebody once had a meal with Henry James, and James muttered, while munching his mutton, that the nursemaid in *The Turn of the Screw* was not nuts – would that be sufficient to conclude that she was not? Internalists, by handing over authority to the author, give primacy to the author's meaning over the meaning of the work, and we are left with no good reason why we should read the work to get the author's meanings rather than, say, the letters of the author (more about the authority of the author in Chapter 4). While externalist theories failed because there did not seem to be any traits or qualities of texts that were exclusive to literature, internalists, by handing over authority to the author potentially made everything the author said was literature into literature.

But have we not forgotten one possibility here: can we not leave it to the reader to decide whether something is literary, and also what the literary qualities are? I think this is probably what we have done, anyway. When I have appealed to 'we' when writing about the definition of literature in this chapter, and used this 'court of appeal' as a put-down for theories or views found wanting, it is a collective notion of 'the reader' I have had in mind. Part of what we want to achieve is an investigation of what 'we' mean by literature.

FAMILY RESEMBLANCE

What if we relaxed our demands a little? Perhaps Socrates and Plato were heading off in the wrong direction when they wanted to find a set of qualities, or even 'the nature', of something to define it. What if Ludwig Wittgenstein, the Austrian philosopher who revolutionised philosophy in the twentieth century, was right to insist that what unifies our application of a single term to a set of phenomena, such as calling works as different as Proust's *Remembrance of Things Past* and a short lyric poem literature, is not a single quality, but overlapping and 'patchy' qualities. Wittgenstein said nothing about the definition of literature, but if we apply his views about definitions to literature, there is not one thread running through the whole tapestry of literature, according to this view, but several features and qualities uniting all the applications of the term. To look for a single unifying quality, the essence of literature, is the result of a mistaken understanding of how language works.

However, there are similarities between most things, as there are similarities between the novels of Conrad and those of the thriller-writer Le Carré, there are also similarities between the latter and the novels of Harold Robins, and similarities between his stories and stories in so-called women's magazines. However, at some point along this trajectory we would want to draw the line and say that while this kind of work may be literature, the other kind is not worthy of the name. The latter is just not 'deep' enough, not complex or innovative enough. The reasons may be many, but the point is that while there are no doubt family resemblances here, what we want to know is which shared qualities are essential for literature, and which are not. We are back, then, with some qualities which we would like to call literary, but where do they reside, and which are they? We shall now look at a theory which tries to answer these questions, and also to avoid the difficulties we have detected in our discussion so far.

AN INSTITUTION-THEORY

The ordinary-language philosophy associated with Oxford in the post-war period is a foundation for Stein Haugom Olsen's theory. A development of this movement was what has become known as speech-act theory. Some of the names associated with this theory are John Austin, John Searle, Sir Peter Strawson and Paul Grice, who were, to various degrees, inspired by Ludwig Wittgenstein.

Olsen thinks that the shortcomings of the kinds of theory we have discussed above can be overcome by an approach inspired by speech-act theory. One common problem for some of the kinds of theory we have discussed is that sentences, passages and whole works are not delivered with instruction-manuals as part of their standard equipment. They do not declare their purposes openly, nor do they tell the reader how they should be read. This means that you may just as well read Conrad's *Heart of Darkness* as a story about a guy who travels up a big river in central Africa, sees quite a few nasty things, meets a questionable character called Kurtz only to have him die on him. Then he goes back to Europe and lies to Kurtz's fiancee. End of story. We do not, however, approach literature in this way, because we have expectations about how these texts should be treated. In other words, we know that these texts are literary texts, and we read them differently from other texts. This means that it is seriously myopic to regard these works as texts only. In order to understand the phenomenon of literature, we have to include the expectations of readers, and the conventions guiding all parties involved in the literary exchange. What Olsen proposes and develops in several books and articles[11] is an institutional theory of literature.

Crucial to his approach is the purpose a reader takes the text in front of them to have, and in particular what is the way to read it if the purpose of the text is a literary one. Speech-act theorists introduced the concept of constitutive rules, which generally have the form 'X counts as Y in the context C'. One non-literary example to illustrate this, is that when the person in black running around on the pitch blows the whistle, this counts as a signal to stop play in the context of soccer. If we eliminated the rules and shared conventions of football, this kind of action would be quite bizarre. Now if we apply this formula to literature, we see that a text can count as literature only if we have conventions and expectations about what literature is and how it is written, published and read. In other words, that the text counts as a literary work given the conventions for reading literature. This means several things. One is that we cannot expect to find some crucial feature in the text alone which by itself makes it literature, nor that the genius of the author makes it so. It also means that we have to negate Derrida's famous dictum that there is nothing outside the text, and say that there is indeed something outside the text, and that this something is vital to making it literature. Texts have purposes, and these vary from one text to the next, and we may of course disregard them completely. However, in the majority of cases disregarding the purpose of a text will carry consequences, and one of these is missing the point. To identify a text as literature is not only about noticing structural features about the text itself, but it is also about relating to it in a way different from how you relate to other texts. Your attitude to a work of literature should be different from your attitude to the newspaper. The article in the newspaper may also contain plot, irony, metaphors and whatever, but they are not generally read as literary works. A newspaper report about a bungled bank robbery, for instance, may have a plot which does not need to follow the chronology of the robbery as it happened, it may use metaphors to make the robbers seem silly, such as calling them the Professor Moriartys (or Professors for short), and keeping this mocking irony throughout by calling the robbery 'the master coup'. The article in the newspaper uses features also used in literature, but the purpose is not to fulfil our expectations of literature, but to present a newsworthy item in an entertaining way. It may even be written to deter criminals: to end up in jail is bad, but to be ridiculed in the newspaper because of your ludicrous incompetence may, in the short term, be worse. To read this imaginary article as a work of literature, then, would be to misunderstand its purpose.

However, the same phenomenon can be reversed. Reading the article as if it was literature does not turn it into literature either. There has to be something in the text to facilitate the reading experience, but this is not an argument against Olsen. His conception of an institution of literature encompasses all aspects of it, including the creation. If the author does not satisfy our general expectations of what literature is, we have to conclude that it is such a poor work that it is not even bad literature, it may not even be possible to classify it as literature at all.

Olsen's emphasis is on the literary response; he maintains that literary interpretation is an active reconstruction of the text, and through this reconstruction the reader defines the experience of the work which makes it an aesthetic experience:

> interpretation of a literary work of art consists in a network of aesthetic considerations. An interpretation is an apprehension of the features of a work which makes it, as a work of art, worthy of a reader's attention. It is . . . an attempt to get out of the work the pay-off which a reader has learnt to expect from literary works.[12]

Olsen provides a detailed account of this process, and its main features are called 'segmentation' and 're-description', in other words: one gives the text a structure different from the one presented in the text. Some features, or passages of the text, are considered more important than others, and it is the identification and individuation of these that Olsen calls 'segmentation'. It is not the case that one sentence is just as important as the next, or that any person or action is as important as the other. Segmentation may involve a realisation that the sanity or otherwise of the nursemaid in Henry James's *The Turn of the Screw* is a major feature, or that windows function as symbols in Emily Brontë's *Wuthering Heights*. When redescription is concerned, this consists of ascribing a purpose to a segment. Examples can include that the said

windows in *Wuthering Heights* represent the boundaries between different
sets of characters and their worlds, that Peer Gynt's ride on the ram in
Henrik Ibsen's dramatic poem of the same name symbolises his virility, or
that the frame narrator in Conrad's *Heart of Darkness* functions to
highlight its fictionality. These redescriptions are only parts of a network
of similar segments and their redescription, where there are ever higher
levels of generality. The highest of these levels is what one takes the work
to 'be about', its theme, that *Heart of Darkness* is about the fragility of the
self, for instance. These very general statements are what Olsen calls
'thematic concepts', and they typically deal with the eternal questions. If
they do not, the themes may be topical, and the work will soon be
'obsolete' since what is topical by its very nature changes fairly rapidly.
The truly thematic concepts are what we might call 'mortal questions' –
the inescapable problems, paradoxes and dilemmas of human existence,
which philosophy also deals with, but in a different way: typically through
argumentation and conceptual clarifications.[13] The end product of the
process of interpretation, which Olsen calls 'appreciation', is the artistic
purpose we ascribe to the author.

This was a quick summary of a theory that is an alternative to the types
of theory we discussed earlier. It is an improvement on these, but by no
means faultless. One problem is that the institution of literature must
have come about somehow: it has not been there from the beginnings of
time, not even from the beginnings of the human race. Olsen goes so far as
to say that:

> apart from the institution of literature there would be no literary works, no artistic
> features, no artistic unity or design, no structural elements, or any other such
> features we recognize as having to do with the aesthetic nature of the literary
> work.[14]

Then the problem is how the first literary work could be produced and
read as literature. Somehow, one imagines, there must be some quality of
the work which made such a reading if not inevitable, then certainly in
some way facilitated by the text. Then we are back with the externalist
models, and Olsen for one would not like that. It does not help much to
argue that the mode of reading literature is inherited from religion,
particularly (in the west) the reading of Christian parables. This only
pushes the problem back one step. It seems likely that some works are
written as literature, presumably after what we can call the literary
institution has been established – when there are a number of people
who explicitly, or more likely implicitly, know how to read and respond to

literature. However, some works can also have the status of literature 'thrust upon them'. They have not been written as literature, but can be read as such. These works yield to this kind of reading, but not only that: the earliest examples may also have been such that they helped the literary response to develop. There were features of these texts which guided readers to respond to them in the way that Olsen outlines, but that would mean that the qualities of the text were present before the literary mode of reading.

This looks a bit like a chicken-and-egg problem. If any author wrote a work with a mode of response in mind which was more or less like the one Olsen outlines, then it was only a matter of getting a public to read it in this way. We have seen previously that in ancient Greece poetry and drama developed out of religious festivals, and it is likely that the telling of stories has been a regular feature of human society since our ancestors developed the ability to speak. But literature is not only stories, it is also a way of making sense of the stories which usually, but not always, involves symbolism, metaphor, complexities of character, and the development of plot. This is just what we started out with: literature is not just fiction, or story, it is a genre most modern human societies value more highly than other fictions or stories. The quality of literature in a country has been a source of pride, Britain champions Shakespeare, and Germany has even named its international cultural liaison department 'The Goethe Institute'. The cultural pride and power thus represented may be seen in many ways, but it tells us that literature is not just any collection of words. The question we started out with was how we could distinguish this most valued set of works against the dross, and we have come to the conclusion that the way we read literature is different from how we treat other texts. This is not enough, however, there have to be qualities in the texts themselves which yield to this kind of approach, too. Olsen claims, then, that literature is constituted by the literary approach, and this is the way of reading applied by the literary institution to literary works. But how can we distinguish this institution from others? Only by its use of the literary mode of reading, apparently. His claim is then that the other ways of reading, be they for historical, ideological, social or other information or insights, are not literary modes of reading. New historicism, for instance, or feminist criticism are both relatively recent and widespread modes of approaching literary works practised by professors and lecturers of literature. These modes of reading focus on social forces and ways in which ideology, in the broad sense, has shaped cultural products, including literature. These examples are not *literary* criticism, according to Olsen because they do not read the works *as literature*. This looks circular, and it is. Olsen identifies the literary qualities as those qualities produced by the literary response, and this response in turn is identified as the response adopted by the members of the literary institution, which is potentially all of us. But this literary institution is distinguished from other institutions by the fact that it employs the literary response to literary works. Olsen admits the circularity, but tries to get out of it by appealing to a set of works we all agree are literary ones. This body of works is called a canon, which is an ostensive[15] definition of what literature is:

> This is a discussion which only makes sense if there is agreement about the existence of a canon. This agreement does not merely concern the fact that such and such texts should be classified as literary works. It is an agreement assigning these texts a cultural value.[16]

Perhaps we may use this to determine if a work is a literary one or not, but the problem is that works go in and out of this canon, and the canon as a concept has been and still is subject to a barrage of criticism from diverse quarters. We started this discussion by pointing out that the very challenges to the canon provide one of the main reasons why literature may need to be defined – or why it is worth our while to test our intuitions about the identity of literature. So, is the fact that there is a disagreement about the nature and content of such a canon proof that the concept of literature has gone down the plughole in recent years? The question is whether literature is an 'essentially contested concept', and also what kind of conceptual creature these concepts are.

LITERATURE:
AN ESSENTIALLY CONTESTED CONCEPT?

In the 1950s the philosopher W. B. Gallie published an article about what he called 'essentially contested concepts';[17] examples of such are 'democracy', 'art' and 'religion', and also sub-classes of these, such as 'parliamentary immunity', 'coloration' and 'dogma', and it should not be difficult to see 'literature' among these, even if Gallie does not use it as an example. Here I shall first discuss this class of concepts in general, and finally see if 'literature' is such a concept, and what implications this may have.

What are the characteristics of essentially contested concepts? The examples mentioned here, and others, are all very general and rather vague, and it is not surprising, therefore, that there is an ongoing debate about their uses. One could be excused for thinking that when informed debaters realise that they are using the concepts differently the debate comes to an end – after all, it is only a verbal disagreement. However, this does not happen, and the debates go on with each side still at loggerheads with the other. Gallie has a long list of criteria of what is an essentially contested concept, but I shall concentrate on the main ones. It is clear that the use of these concepts is appraisive, and that they are used about valued achievements of one sort or another, though the reasons for their being valued highly need not overlap. So, one user of literature as a concept can use it to value aesthetic achievements, while another uses it to value the plot and characters drawn by the author. But one may object that these two sides cannot still be talking about the same thing, and that the concepts are essentially confused rather than essentially contested. The answer to these objections is that no matter how different the views and uses of the concept, there is still an agreement about an original exemplar, or exemplars, whose authority is recognised by all sides in the debate. In the case of literature, this would have to be something like the canon of great works to which Olsen also appeals.

The emphasis on past achievements may be inherently conservative to an unwarranted degree. It seems to imply that what is done today cannot match the greatness of the past. In the case of the Christian religion this may be warranted: nobody can quite match Jesus's exemplar, but in the case of literature this is not impossible. This, anyway, is the line taken by John Kekes in a reconsideration of Gallie's seminal contribution.[18] Kekes argues that what is needed to avoid confusion is that the contestants agree about the general description of the domain they are contesting, and that they share the problem which prompts the debate.[19] This seems to imply that there may be a rational solution to any disagreement about essentially contested concepts, and that if literature is one of these, we may well get a settlement one day. However, I would not put my savings on this outcome, nor would I recommend anybody else to do so.

What is the result of our discussion, then? We may be tempted to substitute 'literature' for 'what is beautiful' in Socrates' conclusion at the end of *Hippias Major* and say that 'what is literature is hard'. We have, however, moved in a circle from where we started. The motivation for even wanting to define literature is that it is no longer taken for granted that literature is a domain it is valuable to deal with, and that the very notion of literature has been radically questioned. Radical social forces have also questioned the values of the established canon of literary works, and asked if it is not just a part of the establishment and thus represents repressive values of patriarchy, and social and cultural power. This background presented the 'why' of defining literature, and when we moved into the 'how' we went back a long way to the beginnings of philosophy in antiquity before moving forward in time to common practices in the contemporary period. The various proposed definitions culminated in Haugom Olsen's theory of a social institution, where literature is a set of shared conventions about the way readers and writers interact in literary communication. While Olsen was subjected to criticism, I should make it clear that in broad outlines his institutional theory is a fruitful starting point for investigations into the nature of literary interpretation, as will be clear from subsequent chapters. However, his appeal to a canon of literature brought us right back where we started: with this canon being questioned. Gallie and Kekes brought us back to the 'how' of definitions, and perhaps to the roots of disagreements. If there is one thing the debates about the nature and qualities of literature show, it is that it matters a great deal to many people. It matters so much, in fact, that it seems almost impossible to agree on what it really is. Perhaps those who hold that 'literature' is too big a collection of diverse discourses are right: they claim that literature is just a convenient way of saying 'poetry', 'drama', 'short stories' and 'novels'.[20] These sub-divisions are much easier to identify and classify according to 'external' markers observable in texts themselves. However, the willingness to use the concept of 'literature' to identify a class or type of text we deal with in quite similar ways is indicative, I think, of a sufficient number of similarities to warrant the pursuit of the definition of literature. The answer, as we have seen here, is contested.

FURTHER READING

A thorough and scholarly work on definition is Richard Robinson's *Definition* (Oxford: Clarendon, 1954).

It is also wise to go to the sources to further one's understanding of a phenomenon. Stein Haugom Olsen is the authoritative source of his own theory. The fullest presentation is in his book *The Structure of Literary Understanding* (Cambridge: Cambridge University Press, 1978), but shorter versions can be found in some of his articles in the collection *The End of Literary Theory* (Cambridge: Cambridge University Press, 1987), in particular 'Defining a Literary Work', pp. 73–87.

Important sources for this chapter were also W. B Gallie's 'Essentially Contested Concepts', *Proceedings of the Aristotelian Society*, 56 (1955–56), pp. 167–98, and the elaboration and amending of the ideas in this essay by John Kekes in 'Essentially Contested Concepts: A Reconsideration', *Philosophy and Rhetoric*, 10 (1977), pp. 71–89.

NOTES

1. Why not define philosophy as well? What philosophy is, is the topic of a whole branch of philosophy, metaphilosophy. While this book does not deal with metaphilosophy, it does assume something about the nature of philosophy, as we saw at the beginning of Chapter 1 where philosophy was described as the mother-subject. It follows from this that philosophy poses and discusses those questions too fundamental and/or general to be the topic of any of the sciences. Philosophy is an activity, and I hope this book will be one example of what it can be.
2. Anthony Savile, in *The Test of Time: An Essay in Philosophical Aesthetics* (Oxford: Clarendon Press, 1982), provides a thorough analysis of what it means that a work of art has 'withstood the test of time'.
3. Plato, *Hippias Major*, trans. B. Jowett, in Edith Hamilton and Huntington Cairns (eds), *The Collected Works of Plato: Including the Letters*, Bollingen Series 71 (Princeton, NJ: Princeton University Press, 1989), pp. 1534–59.
4. See Richard Robinson, *Definition* (Oxford: Clarendon, 1954), pp. 149–92.
5. Immanuel Kant, *The Critique of Judgement*, trans. Werner S. Pluhar (Indianapolis, IN: Hackett, 1987). First published in German 1790.
6. See Jerome Stolnitz, 'On the Origins of "Aesthetic Disinterestedness"', *Journal of Aesthetics and Art Criticism*, 20 (1961–62), pp. 131–43.
7. Monroe C. Beardsley, *Aesthetics: Problems in the Philosophy of Criticism* (New York: Harcourt, Brace & World, 1958).
8. Beardsley, *Aesthetics*, p. 127.
9. Doris Lessing, 'To Room Nineteen', in M. H. Abrams (general ed.), *The Norton Anthology of English Literature*, 6th edn, vol. 2 (New York: Norton, 1993), pp. 2300–23 (p. 2308).
10. Roland Barthes, 'To Write: An Intransitive Verb?', in Richard Macksey and Eugenio Donato (eds), *The Structuralist Controversy: The Languages of Criticism and the Sciences of Man* (Baltimore, MD: Johns Hopkins University Press, 1972), p. 136.
11. The most important ones are *The Structure of Literary Understanding* (Cambridge: Cambridge University Press, 1978) and *The End of Literary Theory* (Cambridge: Cambridge University Press, 1987). The latter is a collection of some of the more important articles. His cooperation with Peter Lamarque, *Truth, Fiction and Literature: A Philosophical Perspective* (Oxford: Clarendon, 1994) is also written from the institutional point of view.
12. Olsen, *The End of Literary Theory*, p. 51.
13. Olsen touches upon these questions in several places, but chiefly in 'Thematic Concepts: Where Philosophy Meets Literature' in *The End of Literary Theory* (Cambridge: Cambridge University Press, 1987).
14. Olsen, *The End of Literary Theory*, p. 81.
15. An ostensive definition is one whereby the meaning of a word or phrase is explained by showing something commonly observable or pointing to it, thus dispensing with the use of words.

16. Olsen, *The End of Literary Theory*, p. 22.
17. W. B. Gallie, 'Essentially Contested Concepts', *Proceedings of the Aristotelian Society*, 56 (1955–56), pp. 167–98, later published as Chapter 8 of *Philosophy and the Historical Understanding* (London: Chatto & Windus, 1964).
18. John Kekes, 'Essentially Contested Concepts: A Reconsideration', *Philosophy and Rhetoric*, 10 (1977), pp. 71–89.
19. Kekes also has other criteria for what is an essentially contested concept, but it would take us too far to go into these here.
20. See for instance Martin Warner, 'Literature, Truth and Logic', *Philosophy*, 74 (1999), pp. 29–54 (p. 48). He does, however, also propose that other types of text may 'become assimilated to "literature" if they exhibit markedly certain excellences traditionally associated with the conventional literary forms' (p. 49).

FOUR

THE AUTHOR: RIP?

It is a truth universally acknowledged that the author or authors make the work by writing it. Or maybe not? While in most cases it is undisputed that someone puts pen to paper, or fingers to keyboard, it is not entirely obvious what being an author entails – the extent of his or her authority over how what is written is understood, for instance. If you write a letter to your sweetheart, any misunderstandings can be corrected, you hope, by a phone-call or other letters clarifying any point which the recipient has misunderstood. This remains one of the rights, perhaps duties, of the letter's author. This is not obviously the case when it comes to literary works. In the previous chapter we saw that we treat different kinds of writing differently, and this seems to be the case also when the authority of the author is considered. Whether Joseph Conrad's *Heart of Darkness* is a journey into the European mind, or an indictment of Belgian colonial exploitation has been the cause of heated controversy. While such disputes do not make a great deal of difference to the world at large, literary critics and other people who care about literature have had quite intense disagreements about similar matters, and would it not be more convenient if they could agree that if the originator can be consulted, he or she would have the last word? Clearly, it is not as simple as that. These questions involve a number of complex issues, some of which it is the purpose of this chapter to examine.

I shall start by presenting an ongoing discussion based in the Anglo-American context, but my main focus will be some radical views on the matter, those of Roland Barthes and Michel Foucault, who both seemed either to believe that the conception of 'the author' was dead, or that it should be gotten rid of as soon as possible. Finally, I shall present a completely anachronistic interpretation of Shakespeare's *The Tempest* as a way into considering the sources of authority for literary interpretation.

AUTHORIAL INTENTION:
WIMSATT, BEARDSLEY AND HIRSCH

When W. K. Wimsatt and Monroe C. Beardsley published their joint article 'The Intentional Fallacy' in *Sewanee Review* in 1946,[1] it was against a contemporary background of literary criticism gone quite author-biographical. Why the biographical emphasis was so heavy is of course difficult to say with precision, but after Freud there was a tendency to see literature as the symptom of the author's mind. This, coupled with a lingering romantic tendency to see the author as a genius who suffered for their art, pulled criticism in the direction of the mind of its originator, rather than the words printed on the page.

With Wimsatt and Beardsley this was to change. Theirs was a hard-hitting article in cut and dried prose which left a lasting impact on literary criticism. When its companion piece, 'The Affective Fallacy' appeared three years later, the authors summed up the intentional fallacy as the 'confusion between the poem and its origins . . . It begins by trying to derive the standard of criticism from the psychological *causes* of the poem, and ends in biography and relativism'. The affective fallacy is the

> confusion between the poem and its *results* . . . It begins by trying to derive the standard of criticism from the psychological effects of the poem and ends in impressionism and relativism. The outcome of either Fallacy . . . is that the poem itself, as an object of specifically critical judgment, tends to disappear.[2]

The attack on both these positions is on behalf of the literary work, which is the focus of interpretation. But it is quite clear that works are ambiguous, and academic critics never seem to agree on what they are 'really about'. The example mentioned above, *Heart of Darkness* by Conrad, is fairly typical. The words on the page cannot do the job since their meaning is precisely what the critics argue over, so which are the criteria we can use to solve such disagreements? One thing which needs to be clear before we can answer this is what the purpose, or purposes, of literary interpretation is.

For E. D. Hirsch, jr.,[3] the best known defender of 'the author', the purpose of interpretations of literature is to be found in the academic context. Academic respectability requires that we must be able to determine what a work means, and the only possible source for this meaning is the author. Hirsch's main point is that meaning is a matter of consciousness, not of words. Words cannot mean anything by themselves, but can do so only if determined by a mind. The words are, after all, only messengers, so when there are disagreements in literary criticism, and there are a lot of them, one would expect that the academic literary critics must be able to tell us what is right. In determining this, there are two main ways to go: to go to the meaning of the author, or to the best meaning. If the latter is not the author's, then it must be the critic's, in which case the critic, and not the author of the literary work, is the author of this meaning. What about ambiguity and vagueness in literary works? Surely, just as in everyday speech, the language in literary works can be vague and ambiguous, perhaps even more so than in ordinary language. Hirsch will have none of it. The meaning must be determinate. Some say that a work can have multiple meanings, and that you may emphasise different parts and aspects of a work, but Hirsch's answer to these is that one pattern of emphases excludes other patterns. The appearance of Hamlet's father's ghost in the play cannot both be important to our understanding of it, and also completely negligible. You cannot therefore decide that the most complex and 'rich' meaning is the best – this may overlook the fact that patterns of emphases must conform, otherwise it cannot be the same meaning. This does not imply that works cannot be complex, but it does mean that there is only one way in which they can be complex: the author's way. For Hirsch, the critic's role is to be a kind of midwife: the critic aids authors in bringing their meaning out into the world.

Beardsley responds to Hirsch, and defends the autonomous text against this intentionalist backlash.[4] Texts are self-sufficient entities and their properties limit interpretations and evaluations. He presents three main arguments against intentionalists such as Hirsch. The first is that there are actually texts without authors, such as computer poems, and these also have a meaning, but of course no authored meaning. The second is that the meaning of a text may change after the author has passed away, but authors cannot change their mind, which means that there is no identity between the two. An example cited by Beardsley is Mark Akenside's poem,[5] where it says 'To spread about him that primeval joy/Which fill'd himself, he rais'd his plastic arm'. 'Plastic' means something different now, some 250 years after Akenside wrote the poem. Words change meaning, and then the poem changes meaning too.

Finally, an author who writes an ambiguous text cannot 'will away' the ambiguity – the text remains ambiguous, which only goes to show that the meaning of the text is not the same as the meaning of the author. Beardsley also claims that we must have an eye on which kinds of discourses we are dealing with, and literature is the kind of writing where we care less about the exact intentions of the author.

I think this takes us to the core of the phenomenon of literary interpretations: what is the purpose of reading literature? There is no use looking for criteria of correct interpretation without some idea of what you want to achieve by an interpretation. This question may have several facets, such as what kind of question it is. Is it an ethical question? E. D. Hirsch claimed in *The Aims of Interpretation*[6] that it is unethical to interpret a literary work with any other purpose than to discover the author's intention. Not to pay heed to the author's intention would be to treat the author as a means only, and not as an end in themselves. What Hirsch forgets here is that it is the author who voluntarily presents a literary work, and thus presents it as an object of interpretation. Literature may be seen as an institution, as we saw in the previous chapter, and as such it is a shared set of expectations and norms. One of these is that it is a type of text which 'allows' different interpretations; it is not like the love-letter example from the start of this chapter. We allow literature to be read and perhaps performed in ways not envisaged by the author. The author has the right to determine what is to count as the work, but not the readings it may give rise to. Imagine an author putting this advertisement in the papers:

> To my readers: those of you who see in my character Bill Waterson in my novel *A Different Kind of Life* a person who is weak and looking for a leader-type to give him direction in life – you're all wrong. What I meant was that he is the kind of character who would allow others to make a claim on his kindness, but this is a strength in his character and not a weakness. So there!
>
> Yours, etc., The Author.

It would be absurd for the author to come to the rescue of readers who have got it wrong. Literature is not that kind of discourse. This is what Hirsch overlooks by presenting his pseudo-Kantian argument about unethical interpretations.

So far, this has shown that even if the author may not have full authority over how their work is read, there remains the idea of a work with some kind of meaning, to which the written words of the author are the best clues. Beardsley did imply that the literary work has some meaning, even if the author had no higher authority than anybody else to say which it was. But some have even denied that there is anything to be called 'the meaning of the text'. Let us have a closer look at the radical views of Roland Barthes and Michel Foucault, assuming for the sake of argument that their intentions can be read from their texts.

THE DEATH OF THE AUTHOR:
BARTHES AND FOUCAULT

The short and elegantly written article in which Roland Barthes comes to the conclusion that the author has followed the example of Nietzsche's God and died, is appropriately called 'The Death of the Author'.[7] When the power of Christianity in the western world was on the wane in the nineteenth century, the German philosopher Friedrich Nietzsche declared that 'God is dead', and Barthes's declaration is clearly an echo of Nietzsche. One reason for linking the death of these two has not been widely remarked on. This is that the main item of reading material at all known to most people in the west until the dramatic increase in literacy and publication in the nineteenth century, was the Bible. The reading of the Bible, and the understanding of this work – and texts sacred in other cultures such as the Quoran, may have been paradigmatic in the approach to texts using similar rhetorical features, such as parables and metaphors. Since the authors of these works are believed to be the deity, the authors' authority cannot possibly be greater. For literary works, part of what we have been led to expect of them is some deeper insight into the human condition. Authors of literary works have been considered sages, and many authors have been held in high regard in their own countries as symbols of national achievement, such as Shakespeare in Britain, Goethe in Germany and Ibsen in Norway. With these expectations, it is not surprising that the view that the truth of any understanding of the work should be grounded in the superior mind that created it was widespread. There are, however, differing views.

The central thesis of Barthes's article is the notion of *écriture*, or writing. It is claimed that in the process of writing, any voice or point of origin is wiped out, so any appeal to the author to clear up misunderstandings is useless. The author is just not there any more. Writing, rather, is the neutral space where our own identity vanishes, and the function of the symbol takes over. In other words: when the author 'dies', writing (*écriture*) is born. This is not only baffling, it is also counterintuitive. That the very act of writing wipes out the writer is clearly meant metaphorically, but this is still a tall order.

Maybe this metaphorical murder of the author is a reaction to a French phenomenon, where students were taught the 'correct' interpretation of literary works in schools and universities until not long ago. This approach to the study of literature was not unique to France, but particularly evident there. The critic Gustave Lanson's *History of French Literature*, published in 1895, and revised and updated by others in the 1950s, and his five volume *Bibliographical Manual of Modern French*

Literature 1500–1900 (1909–14) were the groundworks of orthodox university study of literature in France. Contrary to this tradition, which Barthes calls *lansonisme*, he claims that it is language that speaks, not the author. The author is no more than the writing, language knows a linguistic subject but no person. We should note, also, that when this text was written, the ideas of French structuralism were taken for granted by most leading forces of the French intelligentsia.

Structuralism assumed that cultural artifacts could be studied and analysed as objectively as those of natural science, and that the artifacts are exemplifications of a deep structure which is organised like a language. The working out of this deep structure is the object of the science of structuralism. The basis of this thinking was provided by the Swiss linguist Ferdinand de Saussure in the posthumously published *Course in General Linguistics*,[8] edited from his lecture notes, and the validity of interpretations of this text are, as can be expected, hotly contested.[9] De Saussure was interested in the systematic aspects of language, what made language a system, not in its individual utterances, and structuralists of varying kinds have kept this emphasis on the system over the individual expression. Critics have noted that a general effect of structuralism is that it privileges deterministic and mechanical properties of the system, such as the system of language, to the detriment of individual expressions within it. This element is clearly there in Barthes's 'Death of the Author', but it also points forward to the movements of post-structuralism[10] and deconstruction. The former is a ragbag of theories, but what they have in common is a negative attitude to authority and a clear front against unitary narratives of any kind, be they the grand narratives of history or ideology, or the unity of single narratives such as novels. There are also other views associated with the movement of post-structuralism which we can see at least the germs of in Barthes's article, such as the view that there is no centre in the human mind, there is only a tissue of quotations from whichever sources the subject has come across and assimilated. The person is somewhere in this flow, but there is no unique centre where 'it all comes together'. Therefore, writing does not represent an outside world or the ideas of an author, but it performs something through its own act. The text is just a tissue of quotations from diverse centres of culture, and does not come from the author, just *through* them.

The best known post-structuralist theory is deconstruction, which takes its inspiration from the French philosopher Jaques Derrida, who in 1967 published two books[11] which through the 1970s became very influential on Anglo-American literary theorists, but far less so on philosophers.[12] Just what deconstruction stands for, what it 'is', is far from easy to describe, not least because a fundamental assumption of the theory is that meaning is indeterminate and that truth is non-existent. Deconstructive theories, therefore, by their very nature tend to slip out of any conceptual net you try and catch them in. The roots of deconstruction are also the theories of de Saussure, which makes it clearly post-structuralist, and shows itself in the assumption that the properties of the system of language determine the possibility, or impossibility as the case might be, of meaning. The underlying model is not that persons wish to communicate, and use a language to effect this communication. It is rather that language, and the systemic features of language, determine whether or not communication is possible. The sources of meaning are therefore in the system, and since deconstruction holds that this system is unstable, that there is no final ground on which we can argue for one understanding of expressions of language against another, the best we can do is 'play', since analysis and argumentation are impossible. Given this, just how deconstructionists expect to communicate their theories is not clear, since doing so amounts to a pragmatic inconsistency; that the way something is communicated is in direct conflict with what is communicated.

But deconstruction has had a greater impact on literary theory and criticism than on philosophy, particularly in America where whole 'schools' of criticism have been influenced by it.[13] A deconstructive reading will generally attempt to identify the logic of the language of the text in contrast to what the author has tried to express. It will tease out the implicit presuppositions of the text and point to the (inevitable) contradictions in these. This can happen because, according to deconstructionists, rhetorical features are also features of the texts, even if they go beyond words and sentences. There is, therefore, a conflict between literal and figurative meanings within both literal and rhetorical aspects of a text, and between the two. These conflicts cannot be solved because we do not have anything that can determine the outcome of such conflicts. Nothing in the text can, anyway, and the text is all there is, according to this theory. In this way the text is dissolved, and can mean nothing – or everything, and that amounts to much the same in this context. Since deconstruction holds that there are no meanings to be found in texts, it is also of little importance which texts we approach. For some curious reason, however, most deconstructive readings are readings of works in the canon of established 'great' works, and not, for instance, the employment contracts of the deconstructionists themselves, or to pick another example at random, the United Nations Declaration of Human Rights.

Clearly, adopting this view must have consequences for literary criticism, in that one can no longer claim that the text has been deciphered or interpreted. In fact, even if it is unlikely that he was influenced by Derrida, Barthes writes that interpretation is undesirable because this closes the text against other possible meanings. In this way, Barthes writes, the death of the author makes way for 'the birth of the reader', since with the removal of the dictatorship of the author the reading public won their freedom to make the work mean whatever they like.

So far so good, but 'The Death of the Author' is full of assertions which are left alone without any arguments to support them, and there are few if any caveats to his sweeping generalisations. These make it all the more exciting, of course, but do not make a critical appraisal easier. Fortunately Michel Foucault's 'What is an Author?',[14] published the year after Barthes's article, represents much the same position, and where Barthes is sweeping and assertive, Foucault is more argumentative and thorough. Where Barthes is primarily a literary and cultural critic, Foucault, also French, is an historian of ideas, famous for works such as *Discipline and Punish: The Birth of the Prison* and *The History of Sexuality*.[15]

In 'What is an Author', Foucault claims that writing has an historical connection with death. In Greek heroic poetry the purpose was to convey and thereby keep the immortality of the hero, and in the Arabic *A Thousand and One Nights* the narrator delayed execution by telling stories. Today, however, Foucault like Barthes claims that the causation goes the other way. Through the author's complex use of tropes the connection between the author and the work is broken to the degree that the individuality of the author disappears, and the author generates their own disappearance. Foucault also uses authors such as Kafka as examples, but it seems to me that the writings of these authors undermine his conclusions.

Foucault says that the craft of Kafka makes his individuality disappear, that it cancels him out. This is counterintuitive. Most of us have heard, and even used, the adjective 'kafkaesque'. Dealing with bureaucracy, or being hassled by the immigration officials of a foreign country can make you feel as if you are in a story by Kafka. Telling your friends about experiences such as these, you may well say that they were 'kafkaesque'. The feeling generated by Kafka's particular use of the tropes of writing are therefore easily identifiable as his own, to the degree that the effects generated have acquired his name. It can be argued that far from annulling his individuality, Kafka's craft of writing has ensured his immortality, albeit metaphorical. So maybe the idea of the act of writing cancelling out the individuality of the author is less than convincing, but the main force of Foucault's argument is that the idea of the author as a source and determiner of meaning, which he thinks is passé, has been substituted with other concepts and ideas which keep up the authorial privileges and suppress the importance of the author's extinction.

Unlike Barthes, Foucault thinks that the concept of 'writing', *écriture*, contains so many of the regulative ideas of the concept of the author that it cannot be used. It is not sufficient just to state with Barthes that the author has passed on, we also have to locate the space left, and see which openings this may provide. Certainly in this context, Foucault is more of a philosopher than Barthes in that he thinks it important to analyse the concept 'author' into its constitutive elements. It is a mostly unstated premise of philosophy that our concepts often have different uses and meanings, and that this is a cause of confusion. One such confusion can be found, says Foucault, between the two ways in which the name of the author functions. He claims that there is a difference between the proper name of the author and what he calls 'the author-name', since the latter functions quite differently from the former. As far as the 'name of the author' is concerned, it is a question of who put pen to paper, and what kind of life this person had. It is therefore about a real person's relationship with written productions. The function of the author-name, on the other hand, is that it collects several works under one name, and establishes unity, relationship and mutual explanations. The fact that the discourse has the name of an author, such as Shakespeare, is then used to characterise it, such that it has to be received in a particular way given this special status. The author-name therefore works as a categorisation of a part of a discourse.

We can see this if we consider what difference it would make if we discovered that Shakespeare was not born and bred in Stratford-upon-Avon. This would change our beliefs concerning the person Shakespeare, but it would not make any difference to the function of the author-name as Foucault conceives it. Discovering that the Shakespeare who wrote *Hamlet* did not write the sonnets, on the other hand, would affect the author-name since our beliefs about influences and cross-references would have to be changed dramatically. These would also change were we to discover that Shakespeare also wrote the works attributed to the philosopher Francis Bacon, who lived at the same time.

In the case above of the authorship of *Hamlet* and the authorship of the works of Francis Bacon, the author-name, but not the name of the author, would be changed. These minor thought-experiments have shown that these two concepts, the 'name of author' and 'author-name', have different functions. Foucault has introduced a distinction and shown us other facets of the problems related to authorship. One of the characteristics of the author-name discourse is that it is being owned. Foucault is at his best when making historical points, and his main point here is that authorial 'ownership' of books came about historically together with punishment. Both Barthes and Foucault claim that the author is a modern figure, created as the individual gained value, in other words a product of capitalism.[16] Foucault writes about a 'privileged moment of *individualization* in the history of ideas'.[17]

It is Foucault's historical point that texts and books only got authors in our legal understanding of the term when authors could be punished. Another characteristic of the author function is that it has not affected all kinds of discourses in the same way. Literary works (yes, he has such a category, but drops it quickly as if it were a ticking bomb) were long accepted because their age guaranteed their status, while scientific texts were accepted as true only if they had author names. Around the seventeenth or eighteenth century this changed, according to Foucault, so that scientific discourses were accepted because of their content, while literary works were the ones to gain an author-name if they were seen as acceptable. The implication is that if the modern conception of the author came about through historical forces, then historical forces can also make it disappear again. Foucault does not go deep into any reasons for this, but some tendencies at the time are worth noting.

Scientific methodology became more established in this period, so that the reputation of the scientist mattered less than before so long as the experiments could be replicated. This was the theory's chief claim to truth and acceptance. As for literature, the Renaissance heralded a greater emphasis on the individual, a tendency amplified later by the Romantic movement and its view of the artist as a genius. But what is the relevance of these ideas for our inquiry into the role of the author?

Foucault seems to think that by showing how the author-name works as a classification of the discourse, rather than just pointing to who wrote it, this sense in itself annuls the extensional reference, but that is certainly not the case. That the author-name, such as Shakespeare or Shakespearean, can work in a classificatory capacity, does not show that it cannot possibly also work as a reference to some person who wrote it. Foucault is simply jumping to conclusions. It is probably accurate, however, that the conception of the writer as author, with the attendant rights and obligations, is modern. This is actually a social and legal concept of authorship. The author is seen as an owner of a product, and as having a set of rights and responsibilities with respect to this product. However, this is about real people, as opposed to constructs, and therefore does not support the far-reaching conclusions of Barthes and Foucault. We shall see that these conclusions concern purely impersonal conceptions, such as what to do with works, or the nature of language. It also has no consequences for literary criticism. The crucial point here, for Barthes and Foucault, is that at some stage in history the critical focus was changed over to the personality of the author.

> The image of literature to be found in ordinary culture is tyrannically centred on the author, his person, his life, his tastes, his passions, while criticism still consists for the most part in saying that Baudelaire's work is the failure of Baudelaire the man, Van Gogh's his madness, Tchaichovsky's his vice.[18]

This is really a matter of degree, and varies from critic to critic, epoch to epoch, culture to culture. We should keep in mind that the fact that authors are given rights with respect to their work has no implications for literary criticism. The formalist criticism of the twentieth century existed happily in situations where authors had full rights over their works, as well as enjoying the respect of society. It is also likely that even in the present post-modern times, the author's personality is so valuable to publishers as a marketing tool that the focus on the author, particularly in newspaper-criticism of literature, is likely to be stronger rather than weaker. The seemingly insatiable public interest in personalities and celebrities is such that it cannot be ignored as a means of selling books.

One of the impersonal versions of the author, referred to above, which Foucault introduces is 'the author function'. He claims that it is characteristic of the author function that it does not develop as a spontaneous application of a discourse to an individual, but is rather a result of a complex operation where one constructs a rational being called an author. It is not just a simple case of pointing out who sat down and wrote something, but a matter of constructing a mind that could be the origin of the work one is reading. The author function is attributed through the projections of the operations we make on the text – the features of the text we single out, the connections we make between these, and so on. These vary from time to time, and from one discourse to another. But it is notable that Foucault is assuming much the same as many Anglo-American literary aestheticians about determining the type of discourse, and that the interpretation we arrive at is attributed to the author. Foucault thinks that our conception of the author is reducible to this, or that it is at least a major part of our conception of the author. Moreover, this is the conception of the author which remains, and which he wants to vanish.

According to Foucault, the author-function works as a principle of unity in discourses, since the concept of an author means that at some level or other there must be a unity where contradictions are dissolved or explained away. Contrary to Foucault, I think this may not be the only reason why a unity is projected or found in a literary work. It may be that the reason is not that a conception has become current at a point in history, and can therefore be made to disappear again. It just may be that the reason why we project a unity into a work goes much deeper than this. Just consider our first 'objects' of interpretation: they are the people around us as we grow up, and are not objects but subjects, with their own wishes, moods and personalities. We form views of these, we have an idea of 'what they are like' as people based on our experiences of them. As we grow older these views usually get more sophisticated, as our fund of experiences increases. On the basis of these experiences, and what we hear from other people, we form ideas about people's personalities. If people act differently at different times, if a person we thought to be calm and collected suddenly acts as if possessed, we try to find explanations that keep as much as possible of our former views. Anyway, only in rare and extreme cases (schizophrenia is fortunately a rare disease) do we have to conclude that there is no unity in the personality of a person we know. It is likely that we understand intentional products much in the same way as we understand people, the understanding of people in early life forming the model of how we relate to intentional products such as literary works. If this is the case, the reason why we project unity and coherence – at some level or other – into literary works, is not the result of some ideological imposition, but based in the way we are as human beings. Foucault thought that the tendency to view literary works as coherent was a historical development, but this is not the only possibility. In fact, it may be our 'natural' way of approaching intentional products to assume that at some level or other, they have a unity of purpose. I shall pursue this idea in the next chapter, but now it may be useful to sum up what Foucault's 'author function' is.

First, the author function is tied to the legal and institutional system which determines and articulates the discursive universe. In plain English this means that the author function is an ideological construct which fits in with the power structures in society. Since this means it is not 'natural', it is a complex entity which is not determined by any simple ascription of a discourse to its producer, like 'Shakespeare wrote *Hamlet*', but rather with a series of specific and complex operations. The idea of an author is for Foucault a limit to the meanings a discourse can have, and this is why he thinks that the idea of an author has to be completely changed. The author, according to Foucault, is not an individual who precedes the work, but is rather a function which is used to limit the free circulation, manipulation and composition of works of fiction. The author, therefore, is the ideological figure which marks the fear of the creation of meaning, and for this crime the author should hang, according to Barthes and Foucault.

One may be tempted to ask, with this in mind, why Foucault should bother to read the works of others if the very notion of the work being by somebody is an infringement on the right to make it mean whatever you choose. My suggestion is that one reads the works of others in order to learn something. To write something and put it into the public realm is an implicit claim on the time and effort of others, it says 'I have got something to tell you'. The positing of the work as something which is not yourself or by yourself, implies that it may challenge your preconceptions, that new ideas may have entered your mind during the reading, or that you have had a vicarious experience reading it. The very idea of an interpretation is to give weight to both poles of the notion of '*inter*' – that it takes place between two or more entities. The unquestioned premise Foucault, like Barthes, seems to take to this discussion is that the reader should be free to make any work mean whatever the reader chooses, and that any impediment to this freedom is a capitalist conspiracy. The British Marxist critic and theorist Terry Eagleton joked about 'The Readers' Liberation Front' as a response to the idea of the death of the author, but how does Foucault's own discourse measure up given this premise of unbounded signification? Do we want to make it mean whatever we like?

What we have seen here is that there is a continuum from tying a text to an author on the one hand, and on the other of having a much fuller conception of a classifiable work of a certain type which fulfils a purpose and expresses a meaning. The plausibility of the historical thesis is progressively weakened over this spectrum, since it is not only much more difficult to date the view that works have unity, meaning and value, than it is to date the attribution of an author, but it is also unlikely that there ever was a 'golden age' when unity, meaning and value was *not* ascribed to literary works.

So what we have seen here is that it may well be the case that at some point in history writers became authors in the sense that they had rights and duties with respect to what they wrote. That is for legal historians to decide. It is not proven, however, that to see a text or a work as united and coherent can be dated to the same period. Indeed, all evidence points to this being a more fundamental aspect of understanding intentional phenomena, which is therefore also less likely to disappear.

The presupposition of unity is very deeply rooted, as we can see from a case reported by the neurologist Oliver Sacks in *The Man Who Mistook His Wife for a Hat*.[19] A man suffers from an extreme case of Korsakov's disease, where he cannot remember anything from one moment to the next, and this includes his own identity as well as that of the people he meets. As Sacks writes, 'such a patient *must literally make himself (and his world) up every moment*'.[20] And this patient, Mr. Thompson, makes up not only his own identity but also that of the people he meets. Every time, and with new variations.

> Abysses of amnesia continually opened beneath him, but he would bridge them, nimbly, by fluent confabulations and fictions of all kinds. For him they were not fictions, but how he suddenly saw, or interpreted, the world. Its radical flux and incoherence could not be tolerated.[21]

Thompson simply has to give everyone he meets and himself an identity, and not only that: it has to be an identity and a personality which fits with the facts. Clues are given significance and causal chains are pursued in the hope of finding a unitary interpretation for the intentional world around him. This case of extreme neurological dysfunction just goes to show how important it is to understand and provide a narrative that gives meaning and unity to people. Mr. Thompson's problem is not his desire for a unitary understanding of the world he lives in, but his inability to hold on to it for more than about a minute at a time.

The view Barthes and Foucault became known for in this context is not the historical thesis, but the view that the author is dead. What this death amounts to must be seen in relation to the views inherent in the various conceptions of 'author', some of which are rather obvious, others less so. Whether or not the author is dead depends on what kind of creature he or she was thought to be. As a statement, the death thesis can both be a statement of fact or pure wishful thinking. This is the same kind of ambiguity as in Nietzsche's original death thesis – that God is dead. On Barthes's part it is just a wish, which is made clear when he says that 'the sway of the author remains powerful'.[22] Foucault, on the other hand, says both that we have to locate the space vacated by the vanishing of the author,[23] and also that the author will disappear some time in the future.[24] This authorial limbo of being still alive and quite dead must be seen in relation to the various conceptions of the author that we have been looking at.

It is still the case that the writer-as-author with social and legal status exists. To take an extreme example, authors can still be sentenced to death for what they write, as Salman Rushdie was. Anyway, whether we should want to dispense with the notion of the writer-as-author is a political and moral question in that it is a question of the treatment of real people in a legal and political setting. As for author-based criticism, the death of the author only states that crude author-based literary criticism is dead. This is quite trivial, but only true to a degree in that many readers and a wide section of the media are still very interested in the life of authors. However, in the academic community there is a wide consensus that concentration on the author's life and personality is a dead end, even if biographies of authors, albeit dead ones, is still a legitimate pursuit. That many still believe in 'the death of the author' is probably based on a perceived death of author-based criticism in academia. If they look beyond academia to literary criticism in newspapers and magazines, they will find the focus on the author very much alive.

What about the author function, then? The author function works to establish a determinable meaning for a work or a text, and concerns whether or not qualities such as coherence, expressiveness and creative fantasy are found in literature. The view that these qualities are necessarily implied by the concept of literature is still widespread. In this context it is worth reminding ourselves that the author function is independent of its relationship to any actual person. It is the projection of a creative mind into a text. Foucault would therefore accept that this version of the author still exists, and that it is an ideological product which is repressive and limiting on the creation of meaning.[25] It is this latter conception which is Foucault's main charge. It has little to do, therefore, with the author as person, or even as a role in society, it is rather a prescription for getting rid of a concept of literature, and supplanting it with the free play of the signifier. Rather than a thesis about the emergence of a concept of works having an author in early modern times, we now see that this is a recommendation for how to treat literary works.

The author function, which Foucault attacks, works to ensure that a text is limited in meaning, and provides unity and coherence. This also shows how badly the pieces fit for Foucault. First, the author as person, with a life, a legal status etc., has no place in this conception. That having an author became important for our conception of types of text at a point in history is independent of the view that the text is a unity, and having limits as to what it can mean. The result is that when Foucault postulates the author function thesis he assumes a kind of institutional view like the one we discussed in the previous chapter: the qualities of unity and meaning are not based in an individual, the author, the critic or the reader, but in an institution, incorporating all these in a shared system of expectations. That is, they are collective, common to a culture or a larger collection of people. There is no reason, therefore, to see limits in interpretation, or the source of unity and coherence, as being connected with the author as person. Rather, there is every reason to see these as being shared by a wide community of people, and they are seen by these as 'good practice'. In many ways it is as if Foucault has not quite assimilated his own theory; he writes as if the point of attack is still the author as a person beyond the work. However, his conception of the authored text is defined purely institutionally, and the limits to interpretation, coherence and value, and so on, are determined independently of the will of the author.

Barthes's version, to go back to him for a moment, of the author function is what he calls 'the modern scriptor' who 'is born simultaneously with the text', for 'every text is eternally written *here and now*'.[26] This fits in well with the claim that 'writing is the destruction of every voice, of every point of origin'.[27] The nature of writing makes the author as person superfluous, since in writing there is no function other than the practice of the symbol in itself, and thus the voice loses its origin.[28] This is just a sweeping assertion, but let us for argument's sake pretend that there are such narratives, and that in these cases the focus is turned away from the voice of origin. It does not follow, though, that we can generalise from this case to an all-encompassing thesis about writing. It would be quite absurd to generalise from specific conventions in a kind of fiction to the nature of writing as such, but that is what both Barthes and Foucault do when they claim that writing *as such*, unlike the restricted author text, does not yield any determinable meaning.[29] They claim that writing today has liberated itself from the expressive dimension, it is an interplay of signs and that it is like a game. The argument seems to have this core: determinable meaning is always a product of the pressure of the author, so where there is no determinate meaning there is no authorial presence either. Writing as such (*écriture*) is just a play of signs, so writing as such shows that the author is superfluous. The reasoning here is quite something. It takes for granted that there is 'writing in itself'. *Écriture* is quite simply defined as author-free, to lack any determinate meaning, and to be free from any limiting conditions. The circularity is obvious, since to postulate that there is writing as such, it will have to be author free, lack determinate meaning, and so on. If what you want to demonstrate is present in the assumptions you make in order to demonstrate it, you demonstrate nothing but arrive in thin air.

WHERE IS THE SOURCE OF MEANING?

The idea of the text as an explosion of unlimited meaning, without origin and purpose, is a theoretical fiction. We could, maybe, see a text in this way with some kind of superhuman effort, like hearing a symphony as a series of unconnected sounds. But why bother? It is widely agreed that literary works are interpreted in different ways, and that the same string of words can be construed to have different meanings. But this does not imply that a text can have any meaning whatever. Barthes and Foucault seem to suffer from the misconception that more is better, but quantity and quality are distinct concepts. We need to remind ourselves, after reading Barthes and Foucault, that writing, like speech, is guided by purposes. These can be disregarded, but even if we push the author out of the picture, a series of words are restricted by what these words can possibly mean in the language.

Our exposition so far has shown that while it may be a mistake to identify the meaning of a literary work with the intentions of its author at the time of writing, there must be some limitations as to what the work can mean in order for it to be that particular work. Some kind of identity must be involved. Consider, for example, if we substituted an interpretation of *Hamlet* for one of Emily Brontë's *Wuthering Heights*. It would be plain silly, of course, but if you hold that 'anything goes' this would also have to be possible. Any reference to characters would be absurd since the characters are not the same ones, and this would also go for any reference to action and symbolism. In fact, there would not be much left of *Wuthering Heights* which could be an interpretation of *Hamlet*, and this goes to show that the interpretation must have reference to whatever the interpretation is *of*. But how far can you go without reaching the point of absurdity? Even if we consider only the text and not its origins, we often see that the 'words on the page' have changed their meaning since they were written, a process we may call 'semantic shift'. If a Victorian novelist has one female character saying that she had intercourse with a male character, the present meaning of 'intercourse' is almost exclusively sexual, while for the Victorians it was a social concept in a much less intimate way. Can and should we disregard the original meaning? The example used by Beardsley from Akenside's poem, where a character 'rais'd his plastic arm', was used to show that the text changes its meaning when language changes. But isn't this just an example of how we have to investigate the text's origins in order to understand it? If we do want to understand, we have to try to bracket our own present and reach out to the past to understand it. However, this is not a matter of necessity, it is mainly a matter of what you want your reading to achieve, but some notion of 'words at the time of writing' is probably necessary to our concept of text. Further, can we interpret a work in ways which could not possibly have been intended by its author for historical reasons? To test this latter possibility, I shall present here an interpretation of Shakespeare's *The Tempest*, which Shakespeare could not possibly have intended.[30]

There are many beliefs of Shakespeare and his contemporaries concerning the world we live in that we do not share, and it is likely that we understand the play more in line with our own world view than with that of centuries ago. How we make sense of literary works is properly the subject of the next chapter, but even on the background of our discussion of the author's authority it is fair to assume that in understanding a work of literature we go beyond sentence-meaning and construct an understanding of the whole work which emphasises certain parts of it, and tries to see it in a larger context. This kind of activity is likely to draw on our views of the world we live in, and reflect both personal and cultural concerns.

In *The Tempest*, Prospero is the prime mover of the action, and he uses the esoteric knowledge of his books to create the storm and bring his brother and his entourage to the island. Black and white magic were widely believed in in Elizabethan England, while few do so today. Today, however, science is a much more powerful force of good and evil, and the powers of Prospero in the play will seem to us more in line with the powers of modern science. We may even see in him someone who nearly becomes a mad scientist. For Shakespeare, it would be impossible to see Prospero in this light. A modern audience may therefore see the topical themes of ecology, and the power of science for good and evil, played out in the action of *The Tempest*. We may well interpret the work in ways not even possible for the author. Can this be allowed, and if so, can it be avoided?

Clearly, it can be avoided, or we may at least make an attempt to avoid it. We may study as deeply as we can the world and beliefs of Shakespeare and his contemporaries. We may try to put ourselves in their frames of mind, and to understand the play from this perspective. Scholarship on the English Renaissance is highly developed, and we believe we know a great deal about this period. Try as we may, however, it is unlikely we are able to simply bracket our present beliefs. Elizabethan England will in any case be our version of this period, but the question about whether and to what degree we can put ourselves in the mind-frames of others is a question too complicated to be answered here. But the example of *The Tempest* interpreted in the light of modern science shows that it is, at least, possible to see it thus if an emphasis is put on present concerns, rather than on the range of possible interpretations available to Shakespeare's present. Whether or not this is desirable is a question which can only be answered by reference to what such an interpretation is intended to achieve, relevance to present concerns or faithfulness to Shakespeare's possible intentions.

The author, or conceptions of the author or authors, seem to be here to stay. To most of us other people seem much more interesting than disembodied ideas or words, and this fact, natural or otherwise, will be used both by authors and their publishers to promote books. Most writers, though quite unreliable about the origin of their works, admit that somehow their own experiences form the background for their fictional creations. This is not to say that authors should be the main focus of interest for readers. The institutional nature of literature is such that readers are given a wide berth when it comes to making sense of novels and poems, and plays are produced in different ways all the time. Authors remain quite powerless to force any interpretation on their readers, and in any case the writing of the work should suffice. In some cases the authors want their works to be interpreted in several different ways: it is how these authors conceive of literature and the authority of the author. Consider this example of a play written by T. S. Eliot, *Sweeney Agonistes*. I quote an exchange between Eliot and Nevill Coghill about Rupert Doone's production:

Myself: I had no idea the play meant what he made of it . . . that everyone is a Crippen. I was astonished. Mr. Eliot: So was I. Myself: Then you had meant something very different when you wrote it? Mr Eliot: Very different indeed. Myself: Yet you accept Mr Doone's production? Mr Eliot: Certainly. Myself: But . . . but . . . can a play mean something you didn't intend it to mean, you didn't know it meant? Mr Eliot: *Obviously it does.* Myself: But can it then also mean what you did intend? Mr Eliot: I hope so . . . yes, I think so. Myself: But if the two meanings are contradictory, is not one right and the other wrong? Must not the author be right? Mr Eliot: Not necessarily, do you think? Why is either wrong?

This was to me so staggering a point of view that I could not put it down to modesty. I therefore abandoned this attack for one more frontal. Myself: Tell me, Mr Eliot, who *is* Sweeney? How do you see him? What sort of a man is he? Mr Eliot: I think of him as a man who in younger days was perhaps a professional pugilist, mildly successful; who then grew older and retired to keep a pub.[31]

This discussion concerns a play, and it may well be that authors and playwrights consider plays to be a more 'open' genre than novels or poems. However, it is not necessarily the case that authors are authoritarian when it comes to how we make sense of their works. Obviously, there must be some limits, but those limits have less to do with the mind of the author at the time of writing, than with a shared set of norms as to what can be done with literary works. Some claim, as we have seen structuralists and some post-structuralists do, that meaning is a feature of the system of language, that the nature of language as such is that any attempt at individual expression is doomed from the outset. Barthes claimed that the reader was left victorious at the death of the author, but a much more likely victor given such a fatality is the system of language. Structuralists and post-structuralists tend to see language as a monolithic system, through which individual expression is impossible. Is it not more fruitful to see language as the product of changing and dynamic linguistic practices which all the time serve different purposes? This is how some philosophers of language have preferred to view language.[32] The source of meaning is in the people communicating, not in a monolithic system which is independent of these people and their intentions. This is also the case in literary communication, even if in the case of literature we are less interested in the utterer's intentions than we were in the case of the love-letter example we started this chapter with.

We have moved increasingly closer to assumptions about the nature of literary interpretation in this chapter, and just what we do with literary works when we read and make sense of them is the subject of the next one.

FURTHER READING

Gary Iseminger (ed.), *Intention and Interpretation* (Philadelphia, PA: Temple University Press, 1992), includes edited extracts from the major combatants in the Anglo-American intention debate. Contributors include Beardsley, Hirsch, Joseph Margolis, Steven Knapp and Walter Benn Michaels, as well as more recently written and very illuminating contributions from Colin Lyas and Richard Shusterman.

Peter Lamarque's 'The Death of the Author: An Analytical Autopsy', *British Journal of Aesthetics*, 30 (1990), pp. 319–31, is a thorough analysis of Barthes's and Foucault's views on the authority of the author. Lamarque is particularly interested in revealing their implicit views on the nature of literary interpretation. The article is reprinted in *Fictional Points of View* (Ithaca, NY: Cornell University Press, 1996), pp. 166–80.

Although far from new, Christopher Norris's *Deconstruction: Theory and Practice* (London: Methuen, 1982) is good on the roots of deconstruction in structuralism, and also on its implications for critical practice. Norris has also written a book on Derrida, in the Fontana Modern Masters series, *Derrida* (London: Fontana, 1987).

Many critical accounts of deconstruction and other versions of post-modernism have been published, particularly in the 1990s. Some of these appear not to want to understand the phenomenon, but that cannot be said about Christopher Norris's *Truth and the Ethics of Criticism* (Manchester: Manchester University Press, 1995), where he critically examines the roots and many of the claims of post-modern theory. This is the general theme of several of his books in the 1990s.

NOTES

1. Later anthologised in a number of volumes, such as David Lodge (ed.), *20th Century Literary Criticism: A Reader* (London: Longman, 1972), pp. 334–45.
2. W. K. Wimsatt and Monroe C. Beardsley, 'The Affective Fallacy', in David Lodge (ed.), *20th Century Literary Criticism: A Reader* (London: Longman, 1972), pp. 345–58 (p. 345).
3. E. D. Hirsch, jr., *Validity in Interpretation* (New Haven, CT: Yale University Press, 1967).
4. Monroe C. Beardsley, 'The Authority of the Text', in Gary Iseminger (ed.) *Intention and Interpretation* (Philadelphia, PA: Temple University Press, 1992), pp. 24–40.
5. Beardsley, 'The Authority of the Text', p. 26.
6. E. D. Hirsch, jr., *The Aims of Interpretation* (Chicago, IL: University of Chicago Press, 1976), p. 90.
7. I owe a debt to Peter Lamarque's 'The Death of the Author: An Analytical Autopsy', *British Journal of Aesthetics*, 30 (1990), pp. 319–31, reprinted in *Fictional Points of View* (Ithaca, NY: Cornell University Press, 1996), pp. 166–80. Roland Barthes, 'The Death of the Author', in *Image-Music-Text*, trans. Stephen Heath (London: Fontana, 1977), pp. 142–48. First published in French 1968.
8. Ferdinand de Saussure, *Course in General Linguistics*, eds Charles Bally, Albert Sechehaye and Albert Reidlinger, trans. Wade Baskin (London: Peter Owen, 1960) [1915].
9. See for instance Raymond Tallis, *Not Saussure: A Critique of Post-Saussurean Literary Theory* (London: Macmillan, 1988).
10. Post-structuralism overlaps almost completely with a group of theories also collectively referred to as 'post-modernism'. The self-declared representative of these is Jean-Francois Lyotard in *The Post-Modern Condition: A*

Report on Knowledge, trans. Geoff Bennington and Brian Massumi (Manchester: Manchester University Press, 1984) [1979].

11. These books were *Of Grammatology*, trans. Gayatri C. Spivak (Baltimore, MD: Johns Hopkins University Press, 1976) [1967] and *Writing and Difference*, trans. Alan Bass (London: Routledge, 1978) [1967].

12. An obvious exception to this is the American philosopher Richard Rorty, who in several books shows and acknowledges a debt to Derrida.

13. Such as the so-called 'Yale-school', with J. Hillis Miller, Harold Bloom and Paul de Man as the best known.

14. Michel Foucault, 'What is an Author?', in Paul Rabinow (ed.), *The Foucault Reader* (Harmondsworth: Penguin, 1984), pp. 101–20. First published in French 1969.

15. Michel Foucault, *Discipline and Punish: The Birth of the Prison*, trans. Alan Sheridan (London: Allen Lane, 1977), *The History of Sexuality*, 3 vols, trans. Robert Hurley (Harmondsworth: Penguin, 1984–88).

16. Barthes, 'The Death of the Author', p. 142.

17. Foucault, 'What is an Author?, p. 101.

18. Barthes, 'The Death of the Author', p. 143.

19. Oliver Sacks, 'A Matter of Identity', *The Man Who Mistook His Wife for a Hat* (London: Picador, 1986), pp. 103–10.

20. Sacks, p. 105.

21. Sacks, p. 104.

22. Barthes, 'The Death of the Author', p. 143.

23. Foucault, 'What is an Author?, p. 105.

24. Foucault, 'What is an Author?, p. 119.

25. Note here how I write as if Foucault still exists – presumably as the locus of the views expressed by his text. The author function of Foucault still exists, even if the person is dead.

26. Barthes, 'The Death of the Author', p. 145.

27. Barthes, 'The Death of the Author', p. 142.

28. Barthes, 'The Death of the Author', p. 142.

29. Barthes, 'The Death of the Author', p. 146, and Foucault, 'What is an Author?, p. 102.

30. For a complete version of such a reading, with a discussion of its implications for literary interpretation, see Ole Martin Skilleås, 'Anachronistic Themes and Literary Value: *The Tempest*', *British Journal of Aesthetics*, 31 (1991), pp. 122–33. Reprinted in Donald Keesey (ed.), *Contexts For Criticism*, 3rd edn (Mountain View, CA: Mayfield Publishing, 1998), pp. 181–9.

31. Nevill Coghill, 'Sweeney Agonistes', in Tambimuttu & Richard Mach (eds), *T. S. Eliot: A Symposium* (London: Frank & Cass, 1965), pp. 82–7 (p. 86).

32. The late Ludwig Wittgenstein, in *Philosophical Investigations*, trans. G. E. M. Anscombe (Oxford: Blackwell, 1953) can be seen as an advocate for such a view, and so can Donald Davidson, particularly in 'A Nice Derangement of Epitaphs', in Ernest LePore (ed.), *Truth and Interpretation: Perspectives on*

the Philosophy of Donald Davidson (Oxford: Blackwell, 1986), pp. 433–46, where he rejects any view of language as determined by rules. An introduction to Donald Davidson's philosophy of language can be found in Bjørn T. Ramberg, *Donald Davidson's Philosophy of Language* (Oxford: Blackwell, 1989).

FIVE

HERMENEUTICS AND INTERPRETATION

Is Herman Melville's novel *Moby Dick* just a plain tale of whaling? This question will seem silly to anyone with more than a nodding acquaintance with literature. One of the fundamental common assumptions of the institution of literature is that there is something below the surface of character and action. Most critics, and probably readers, have seen the whale in *Moby Dick* as more than just a sizeable aquatic mammal. It symbolises something, but this 'something' is just what critics may disagree about. In this chapter we shall look more closely at how readers make sense of literary works, how this sense-making may be different from how we make sense of other written productions. The main focus will be novels, but using theatrical productions as a public interpretation history in order to evaluate the role of the social and historical context in how we make sense of literary works. This will lead us into a discussion of philosophical theories of interpretation, chiefly the hermeneutics of Hans-Georg Gadamer.

When do you read, and when do you interpret a work of literature? In everyday language the term 'reading' may be more widely used than 'interpretation', but in the academic context they seem to be interchangeable. In the example of *Moby Dick*, the symbolic significance of the whale is typically a point of interpretation. It is a matter of what you make of it, and how you integrate your understanding of its significance with the whole work. In the following, 'interpretation' will be used about the process of coming to an integrated understanding of the literary work. Just a summary of the plot and who the characters are will not amount to an interpretation, but interpretations can be produced at both high and low levels of complexity. To warrant the name of interpretation, an attempt to explain the features of the text which go beyond sentence-meaning must be made, so an understanding of *Moby Dick* as a plain tale of whaling will either not be an interpretation, or a very daring one: claiming that the work is a challenge to shared conceptions of what literary works are supposed to do.

But how do readers *in fact* make sense of literary works, how do we perform interpretations? An answer to this may well come from your own experience of reading works of literature, but the problem is that it is difficult to be both actively interpreting a work, and at the same time be the outside observer of what you are doing. We may be well able to state the 'result' of an interpretation of a work, saying what it is about and how you justify this, but it always proves just about impossible accurately to recreate the steps taken to get there. Forgetfulness and idealisation come in as distorting elements once we try to step back and make explicit something we did implicitly, and it is in any case not theoretically reliable to use introspection to verify a theory since theories should be inter-subjectively valid and not applicable to one person only. We therefore need some kind of objective approach, even if this proves difficult to achieve.

Most of those who have theorised about literary interpretation have used published literary criticism to exemplify how we make sense of literary works. The problem with published works of literary criticism is that what we read in them is the conclusion of the interpretative activity. We want to know how the reader makes sense of a work while actually reading it, even if a full account of this may be impossible to achieve, not how it is presented to others once the reading is over. Published literary criticism is also distorted by the requirements of publishing. Readings of entire novels, for instance, are very rarely published. What you can have some hope of getting published are new and preferably daring inter-pretations of aspects of literary works. What is published must present something new, the space available is limited, and the presentation cannot follow the path of discovery. The published interpretation is given in a context of justification, where the author justifies the interpretation arrived at, and not in the context of discovery. The result of these and other factors is that published literary criticism bears little resem-blance to how people make sense of literary works, and published literary criticism tells us at least as much about its own genre of writing as about literary works. Granting this, can we ever catch something so fleeting and subjective as the processes by which we treat literary works? Maybe not, though we shall look at a plausible model later in the chapter. What we can do, I think, is identify some major factors in how we appropriate literary works, how we make them our own.

If we go back as far as to how the Christian Bible became 'the good book', that is before the text was ossified into the canonical books, we can witness a process which is quite instructive – the process is called *midrash*.[1] This process is more interpretation than commentary, since to communicate the content to new generations and groups, editors cut, added and changed texts. The object was to minimise the barriers to understanding for groups of people new to the work, and the editing and confabulation was an interpretation of the work's content, not its form. What was edited away was what had become, over the years, offensive or incomprehensible, but things that could make it more acceptable or emphasise important points were also added. Sometimes the stories were expanded with new episodes and actions, maybe even new characters. These additions were always in the service of the content, or 'the message'. This shows that texts, at least prior to our time, are not hewn in stone. In the beginnings of literate culture, texts were not seen as given, but only as media for an underlying 'message' – a kind of meaning which could be put across in several ways, and which had to be put across in different ways given that circumstances change and that different publics must be addressed. The interpretative activity is not done to serve a tyrannical text, but before a public where the text had to give way for the purpose of the text. Communication was more important than the exact nature of its medium.

THEATRICAL PRODUCTIONS AS PUBLIC INTERPRETATIONS

This phenomenon is given little attention in literary interpretation today. However, a similar process is still prominent in productions of plays. Like academic literary criticism, the production is an end product of the process of interpretation. But there is no justification, just an attempt to appeal to the public. The individual reader may approach the work in the same way as the producer,[2] but the producer of a play displays their interpretation to a wider public, thus giving us an interpretation which is public without the factors distorting academic interpretations. However, theatrical interpretations considered as literary interpretations also have their drawbacks. David Ward remarks that: 'the play moves on so rapidly, in the real time of performance, throwing up different hints, suggestions, ghosts of allusions, that we're not allowed to dwell on any one lead for long enough to make complete sense of it.'[3]

There are, no doubt, differences between how you approach the literary work when you curl up in the privacy of your own home with a book and a nice cup of tea, and when you sit in an audience watching a play performed before your eyes. In the latter situation there is less or no opportunity to reflect or to flick back and read a passage again. On the other hand, the private reading situation will not give the reader the immediacy and the vivid sense of colour, sound and smell of the theatrical

performance. The question, then, is what this can tell us about interpretation of literature. We have less opportunity to go back to elements of
the work and reassess their significance in the unfolding totality of the
work.[4] However, in presenting the play choices will have had to be made
out of many possibilities, effectively amounting to an interpretation. The
phenomenological situation of performance, and the fact that a production is an interpretation of the play, together mean that the power of the
theatre to challenge the audience's preconceptions is strong in relation to
the reading situation, where readers have greater freedom to accommodate their preconceptions. While the presented play does not 'close' the
possibilities of different interpretations of the performance, the spectator
situation, as Ward points out, does not invite the close scrutiny often
involved in academic interpretations of the written work. No doubt this is
one reason why very few, if any, well known academic interpretations of
plays have been based on performances rather than the text of it, often
leading to a lack of attention to the theatrical aspect of plays.

These considerations merely confirm the common assumption that
producers, with varying degrees of input from actors and others,
present their interpretation of the play and thus take, with respect to
creativity, the place of the reader in the reading situation. For us these
considerations have an interesting consequence: we do not have to go
to particular readers to find what they have made of the play, for the
theatrical performance is itself an object of study sufficient for this
purpose. This has the further advantage, of course, that a theatrical
performance is a public affair and also, in most cases, a commercial
venture. It follows that the interpretation of the play has to appeal to
the public of the day. Thus, though we should be wary of drawing
quick conclusions on this point, we may be able to see from the public
appeal of productions which interpretations have focused themes with
an appeal to the public. Theatrical openness, and hence variation
under the 'control' of tradition, is only a more public manifestation of
a matching openness in the reading and interpretation of plays and
other literary works.[5] Readers have as much, if not more, control over
what they decide to make out of the characters of a literary work, their
voices, personalities, looks and other variables as the producer has,
elements which are no less central to the reader's interpretation of the
work than to the producer's. Similarly, which parts of the text are
seen to be the crucial ones will depend on the interpreter's situation
and concerns, whether reader or producer. According to the well-
known producer and director Jonathan Miller:

Each generation tends to regard certain lines as the crucial ones, but that is because that generation has decided to focus upon one particular plane of interest or meaning within the play, and within that plane certain lines obviously assume a dazzling precedence.[6]

Given this picture, I find the performance history of a play to be of particular significance. It is a public interpretation history with one important difference from that of other literary interpretations: the performed performance must be found valuable by a sufficient number of the paying public, thus having to appeal more to the *Zeitgeist* than a private reading or a literary critical work has to do. The cultural climate also creates a set of assumptions it is hard, if not impossible, for the producer to go beyond. Jonathan Miller displays the theatrical attitude when he argues, in a rather 'purple passage', that fidelity is not the right approach for the producer:

The job of the artist in the theatre is illumination and reconstruction and the endless task of assimilating the objects of the past into the interests of the present . . . Literary and dramatic matter is being continuously created out of fundamental substance created in the early history of the literary universe.[7]

Miller's experience of directing Shakespeare is revealing also with respect to how individual readers make sense of literary works. The theatre, as we have seen, is subject to the influence of its audience. This implies that the interpretations it stages have to appeal to the audience in different ways. This is similar to the reading situation. The individual reader is no more restricted than the producer in what to make of, for example, characters, what they look like, in what manner they speak and 'what it is all about'. Likewise, only more directly, will what readers make of the literary work be guided by their concerns and their situation. If I am right in this line of reasoning, what actually happens in literary interpretations that are not controlled by the criteria of academic literary criticism may be more concerned with the relevance of the work to the reader or the audience than with textual accuracies and subtleties.

THE CASE OF *THE TEMPEST*

When we look at the performance history of a play such as Shakespeare's *The Tempest*, we see that the changing concerns of different historical epochs are clearly reflected in it. The success or failure of a production was very much in the hands of the paying public, and to fail to appeal to the imagination of the public was financially and therefore also professionally perilous. A problem for any study of the performance history of a play is the elusive nature of performances. This is, probably, the reason why literary critics and theorists usually refer to the text of the play rather than to actual performances. There are, we know, several versions of many of Shakespeare's plays. We have folio and quarto versions, and learned philologists disagree about which versions should have priority. Quartos are usually earlier versions or copies pirated from performances which have been improved and then ended up as the folio version, which was published in 1623, long after Shakespeare's death. In these cases it is fair to say that the play existed prior to the text. Work pressures in the theatre of the time was high, and plays were often not written out prior to performance. *The Tempest*, for instance, was performed several times prior to 1623 (first in November 1611), but probably amended a great deal, including the addition of detailed stage instructions. On the basis of these performances, and some textual material, the folio version of 1623 was made. It is arguable that the play, and the reactions it was met with from the public, made the text – rather than the other way round. Further, in the case of *The Tempest* we have access to a number of complete rewritings of the play. While these are not necessarily reliable guides as to how the play was on stage, they still offer an opportunity to look closer at different conceptions of what the rewriters thought were the valuable features of *The Tempest*.

One of these rewritings was done by John Dryden and Sir William Davenant and called *The Tempest, or The Enchanted Island: A Comedy*,[8] first published in 1670. Less than a third is kept of Shakespeare's play, and much is added. Most productions of the Shakespearean classics are cut, leaving out sections of the text for various reasons. In *The Tempest, or The Enchanted Island: A Comedy* the cuts are indeed evident, but more interesting, perhaps, are the additions. Most significant are the new characters introduced by Davenant and Dryden. They are Hippolito (a boy who has never seen a woman), Mustachio, (Stephano's mate), Ventoso, (a mariner), Dorrinda (also a daughter of Prospero who has never seen a man), Milcha (a mate for Ariel) and, of course, a sister to Caliban with the same name as his mother, Sycorax. As one might guess from these additions to the cast, Davenant and Dryden were particularly concerned to explore 'the encounters of innocent love'. In fact, the four characters of Hippolito, Ferdinand, Dorinda and Miranda very nearly take over the play and Prospero, by most critics of Shakespeare's text seen as its central character, is left with a less prominent position in the play. So popular was their adaptation that the original was not again seen on the London stage until 1746, when it ran for only six performances. In comparison, the Davenant and Dryden adaptation was performed 180 times (thirty times more than the original) in the period 1700–50.[9]

Another interesting development in productions of *The Tempest* occurred towards the end of the Victorian period. This was the changing conception of the character of Caliban, which was in part influenced by the work of Darwin, but also, one might surmise, by the development of Great Britain as a major colonial power. The clearest example of this kind of influence is Frank Benson's Caliban in his 1891 production of *The Tempest* for the Stratford Festival. Benson saw the role of Caliban as so important that he starred in it himself. The basis for his conception of the role was a book published eighteen years previously: Daniel Wilson's *Caliban: The Missing Link*.[10] In the introduction Wilson presents his intention thus:

> The leading purpose of the following pages is . . . to show that [Shakespeare's] genius had already created for us the ideal of that imaginary intermediate being, between the true brute and man, which, if the new theory of descent from crudest animal organism be true, was our predecessor and precursor in the inheritance of this world of humanity.[11]

In the chapter 'The Monster Caliban', Wilson says that:

> There was obviously something marine or fishlike in the aspect of the island monster. 'In the dim obscurity of the past', says Darwin, 'we can see that the early progenitor of all vertebrates must have been an aquatic animal'. . . . In Caliban there was undesignedly embodied, seemingly, an ideal of the latest stages of such an evolution.[12]

Benson kept close to Wilson's conception, studied the behaviour of great apes, and gave a very athletic performance as Caliban. According to Mary M. Nilan,[13] Benson played Caliban on all fours, made up to look like an ape and 'always entered with a large and very real fish clenched between his jaws'.

In Shakespeare's play, Prospero comes to the island, the victim of a coup in Milan, empowered with the force of magic and puts the two inhabitants, the spirit Ariel and the 'salvage and deformed slave' Caliban to work for him. He maintains his power by threats, punishment, promises and by his superior knowledge, most potently realised in his magic. The two subjects are indeed different, which is reflected in their attitudes to their master. Ariel is compliant, though he repeatedly asks his master to be set free. Caliban, on the other hand, claims right to the island by his mother, the witch Sycorax, and hatches, together with the two ship-wrecked fools a plot to overthrow Prospero. Not least this latter fact, together with Caliban's claim that the island is his own, has inspired third-world critics and dramatists to portray him as the oppressed native struggling to break free of the oppressor from a developed country.

Of these Aimé Césaire's *Une Tempête* (1969) is perhaps the most illuminating example. It is worth noting that the title of Césaire's play has the indefinite article; it is implied that this tempest is only one of many, because wherever and whenever there is oppression, there will be a 'tempest' to overthrow the oppressors. Césaire is a novelist, playwright and politician of Martinique in the West Indies. He has been very clear and outspoken about his intentions in writing *Une Tempête*, which had its world première at the Festival of Hammamet in Tunisia.[14] Césaire wanted to 'de-mythify' *The Tempest*, and continually broke away from the original in making his own version. His justification for this is that a great work of art, such as *The Tempest*, belongs to humanity and as such can undergo as many reinterpretations as the myths of classical antiquity.

In a way, what Césaire has done with Shakespeare's *The Tempest* has a parallel in the abridged versions of Shakespeare produced for foreign speakers. The cuts he has made have thus a double genesis; one in the time-honoured theatrical practice of cutting dialogue from plays for the purpose of performance, and the abridgement made so that the classics will be easier to understand for foreign speakers of the language. This latter parallel is perhaps the most instructive, since the gaps have been filled, not with elaborate explanations but with the discourse and political reality of the day: Ariel does not use magic or song to coerce the plotters, but riot-gas. Gonzalo wants to keep the island unspoiled for tourists to enjoy. The spaces opened up, Césaire has filled with the culture and political concerns of its audience. The western icon of culture, Shakespeare's *The Tempest*, is cut open and filled with the self-understanding and concerns of a different culture.

So, what can we learn from these short glimpses from the performance history of *The Tempest*? I am suggesting that when reading novels and short stories, let alone plays, readers make sense of the works in ways similar to how producers create productions of plays: by making them relevant and interesting to the audience. This process is not one-sided, in that there is an interplay between the literary work as such, and the life, mind and concerns of the reader. The work is open to different and differing realisations. As we have seen with *The Tempest*, one epoch focuses on one aspect of the work, and even readers from different countries or with different interests read the work differently, as we have seen in the case of Césaire's production.

GADAMER AND HERMENEUTICS

At the end of Chapter 4 the question of the source of meaning was discussed. For structuralists and their intellectual descendants meaning was a feature of the system of signification, while for intentionalists like E. D. Hirsch its true genesis was only in the mind of the writer. Our journey in this chapter, from the question of how we actually make sense of literary works, through the performance history of *The Tempest*, has shown that the meaning of a literary work is worked out in the meeting of a text with the active mind of a reader. If these examples from theatrical productions are relevant also for the reading of literature in prose, which I suggest they are, it cannot be the case that the reader recreates only the meaning an author wills into the text. Interpretation is not just decoding something the author encoded while writing the text. The meaning is created at the meeting between texts and the minds of readers. Just one of the parts of this meeting cannot dictate the outcome, no matter how important the reader thinks the recovery of the original meaning is.

Fortunately, we have a theory and also a philosophy of textual interpretation called hermeneutics. Hermeneutics may have gotten its name from the Greek god Hermes, who was the god of thieves, traders, travellers, and of what the heralds proclaimed – their *kerygma*.[15] Hermes is cunning, sometimes violent, and a bit of a confidence-trickster. Given this picture, it may not be surprising that he is also the god and protector of interpreters. Hermeneutics has its roots in the interpretation of sacred scripture, but also in relation to other texts, particularly law. The main philosopher of hermeneutics in the twentieth century has been Hans-Georg Gadamer, whose *Truth and Method*[16] has become one of the most important books of philosophy in the past one hundred years. Gadamer was a pupil of Martin Heidegger, who in *Being and Time*[17] laid the ground for philosophical hermeneutics as distinct from methodological hermeneutics. In this perspective, understanding is not a question of a chosen methodology which is designed to reveal the truth. Rather, understanding is a fundamental mode of being since we are always engaged in our being, thrown, as we are, into a concrete situation we interpret according to our own life and the possibilities it contains. What Heidegger revealed, according to Gadamer, was the fore-structure of understanding, that the interpretation we have of ourselves and our situation is always dependent on a series of conditions we can never exhaustively account for. This is not a methodological demand on the practice of textual interpretation, but 'a description of the way in which interpretation through understanding is achieved'.[18] As we shall see shortly, the 'hermeneutic circle' was already part of the terminology of textual

interpretation, but Heidegger founded this insight in the most fundamental aspects of being rather than as a methodological tool.

Truth and Method argues against the objectifying tendencies in the
humanities which try to recreate an original meaning in its proper
historical context. For Gadamer this is all wrong, since to understand
something historically is to overlook its possible truth *for us*. The
recreation of historical otherness paradoxically makes it uninteresting
for us at our time, since the text's claim to truth is not taken seriously, but
is only seen as a product or a symptom of its time. Rather, to understand a
text we have to see it as an answer to a question, since all understanding is
dialogical in this way. While it is usually impossible to recover the original
question, we have every possibility to enter into a conversation with the
text ourselves, if we open up to its claim to say something true. This
conversation between text and reader is not one that can be controlled by
either party, but a process which may surprise the reader. So while
Gadamer argues that we always have prejudices, or pre-judgements, when
reading texts, these are inevitable given the fore-structure of understanding, and these form the background of which the text may make the
reader aware. We should note that these prejudices are not necessarily of
the odious kind, but are inescapable aspects of the phenomenon of
understanding.

Gadamer writes that he wants to rehabilitate 'prejudices', which is a
deliberate provocation on his part. He claims that the greatest prejudice of
the Enlightenment was its prejudice against prejudice. Gadamer's usage is
grounded in its original meaning of *pre*-judgement – a judgement or
opinion which is prior to any direct encounter with a phenomenon, thing
or text, for instance. We may never realise that our prior judgements, or
prejudices, exist before our encounter with their objects show them up as
false. It is these judgements, whether we become aware of them when
they turn out to be false, or whether we remain unaware of their existence
since they go unchallenged, which together make up our horizon of
understanding. This horizon will change, 'melt together with the horizon
of the text', and together these will constitute our new understanding.

The upshot is that understanding will always take place against a
background of a pre-understanding. We never meet phenomena as a
tabula rasa, but we may ask what keeps us from just going ahead with our
pre-conceived notions. The key here is that Gadamer claims that our
reading of texts is a conversation with them. To converse you also need
something to talk about, and it is this subject-matter (German: *Sache*)
which is the common focus of the reader and the text. The purpose is to
gain a deeper understanding about this subject matter. This conversation

has its own dynamics apart from those who engage in it. It is not so much those taking part who are 'having a conversation', as it is the conversation which 'has' them, in a manner of speaking. The common pursuit of understanding between text and reader, an understanding of a subject matter or a theme, throws up new insights which in their turn lead to unforeseen territory. Well, this may seem like just some florid use of metaphors, but it emphasises that reading cannot be just a case of taking your hobby-horses out for a ride: your conversation partner, the text, asserts its own claim to truth, and your rationale for reading it is to learn something from it.

One prejudice in Gadamer's sense which we normally have is that we should learn something, that we expect something from the text in front of us, and we may expect something more or less specific. Further, it is not the case that a reader's background, personality and concerns disappear the moment a text is picked up. The reader is a living and active being, not just a function of the text or a self-sufficient ego without any attributes. In order to make sense of the text, the reader will also have to integrate it in his or her language, which means that the reader's present concepts are those into which the historical text will have to be accommodated. When this is taken into account, we see that the source of meaning is the encounter between reader and text, where the reader uses memory, personality and concerns actively. All this is the productive ground of understanding, and the background for the conversation with the text.

There are features of the text which are going to be seen as more significant for a reader or spectator, and these form a unity which becomes the work for this particular reader or spectator. All this cannot happen unless readers are active in their reading. The personal situation of the reader is the productive ground of understanding, which is also emphasised by Gadamer as he insists that the case of law is particularly instructive when analysing the nature of interpretation. What practitioners of the law have to do, is to apply general laws to particular cases. Only when you see that the general law applies to the particular case do you understand the law. Laws are not primarily to be understood historically, but gain their significance through their use in present situations. 'It is only in all its applications that the law becomes concrete'.[19] Gadamer contends that this also goes for philosophical as well as literary texts: ' we do not have the freedom to adopt an historical distance towards them. It will be seen that here understanding always involves the application of the meaning understood'.[20]

THE NATURE OF INTERPRETATION

Still, there is nothing in this which keeps anyone from wanting the interpreter to be as neutral as possible, or to endeavour the highest possible degree of disinterestedness, but the risk in adopting objectifying approaches in the humanities is that we ignore what the texts are saying. Gadamer mainly wants to lay bare the conditions for understanding which are always already there, conditions which cannot be removed by pure volition. Gadamer's hermeneutics, and its inherent plausibility, gives us reason to think that the reader is active in relation to the work, unless the text openly surrenders to outside criteria of one kind or another. It is here that the evidence from the performance history of *The Tempest*, not to mention the more recent productions seen in relation to other cultures, runs together with Gadamer's deeply philosophical and principled considerations. It is hard to avoid the conclusion that the background to interpretations, be they historical or cultural, will matter to interpretation. It certainly does in the theatre, which has to compete with other entertainments for the attention of the public. The question is whether it does so in relation to texts perused in private by the individual reader.

It should be no surprise that I think it does, but such a conviction may easily lead into conceptual traps, which are thick on the ground in this area. What we have established is that we have strong indications pointing in this direction, but it may still be so that the theatrical example is too special to warrant such a conclusion in the case of the private reader in the easy-chair reading a novel. And, let us not forget, it may be that we are constrained by normative restrictions that will force us to seek to over-come the Gadamerian constraints to situations and circumstances.

It is clear that contemporary 'horizons' have mattered throughout the production history of *The Tempest*, at least, and it is my contention that the same kind of application is significant not only from one historical epoch to the next, but also in the case of individual readers with their individual histories and concerns. This may apply to the 'grand level' of interpretation, but how do we as readers make sense of the work as we go along? Here we encounter the problem that we started this chapter with: how to observe yourself while being in the middle of an attention-demanding activity. What most theorists of interpretation seem to agree on is that understanding is a kind of circular activity. This applies all round, not only to the reading of literary works. The German herme-neutic philosopher Friedrich Ast, at the beginning of the nineteenth century, coined the term 'hermeneutic circle' for this insight, that the understanding of the whole is dependent on understanding the individual parts, and that understanding the parts is dependent on understanding the whole. The hermeneutic circle, obviously, is also an inherent feature in Gadamer's hermeneutics.

Let us look at how it may apply to the interpretation of, say, a novel. You have a somewhat foggy idea of what it is all about, based, perhaps, on what you have read in the blurb or heard friends say about it. You attach significance to characters, events, setting and other aspects of the work based on this prior judgement of the whole. But as you go along, you may find that you have judged the significance of a character wrongly, or you suddenly become aware of a pervasive metaphor. Suddenly you see the river in Conrad's *Heart of Darkness* as a metaphor of destruction, for instance. This has consequences for your understanding of the whole of the work, and this modified understanding of the whole work then works as a guide to understanding what you have left of reading it. While this suggested model is highly simplified, it fits in well with Gadamer's highly general claims about the fundamentals of understanding.

This may or may not be the way any one of us approach literary works, and it is, for reasons stated, difficult to know. But I believe in this general model, at least as a picture of how 'educated' readers read novels, short stories and probably plays.[21] While Gadamer's philosophical hermeneutics is supposed to apply to the phenomenon of understanding,[22] more detailed models, such as that of Stein Haugom Olsen, have been developed to apply to literature, or to 'the literary institution' as he calls it. This institution seems to have both implicit and explicit conventions, some of which we discussed in Chapter 4.

The crucial feature of Olsen's model is that we read literature differently from the way we read other kinds of text, which is a point even Foucault accepted.[23] Olsen emphasises that we read literature in a way which is dissimilar to the way we read other types of text, which defines literature according to the expectations and conventions operating, and which makes the work a literary one because it is written and produced on the basis of such expectations. We do not have to read literature in a particular way, but there are good reasons for doing it still.[24] If we did not, we would perhaps see Melville's *Moby Dick* as a plain tale of whaling. The literary way of reading, in short, works so that parts or aspects of the work are given implicit descriptions which are not necessarily taken from the work itself, but which are grounded in concepts which are current or central to the culture or the language. At the lower levels of description these may be suggested by the text, but not necessarily. The role of these in the work will gradually be connected through more general descriptions, which again tie the important aspects of the novel or poem together in a description which gives the work an identity through what it is about. This 'about' is usually some general theme in the culture, or a basic question of human existence, what the philosopher Thomas Nagel calls 'mortal questions'. It would be silly, Olsen claims, to call the result of the interpretation the 'meaning' of the literary work, 'for what would one expect as an answer to a question like, "What is the meaning of *Macbeth*?".[25] He further maintains that this usage is potentially distortive, but I have kept to this usage here because this is the prevalent usage among students and teachers of literature.

We should have a look at how this literary mode of reading may operate in a literary work known to many. In Joseph Conrad's *Heart of Darkness* there is an episode where the 'inner narrator'[26] Marlow's description and seeming admiration for the accountant at the outer station is in conflict with Marlow's disgust and condemnation of the colonial company the accountant serves so faithfully. In this novella, Marlow gets a berth on a riverboat on the Congo[27] after a long time ashore. In the Congo he is witness to extreme greed and callous destructiveness on the part of the European colonists. While at one of the stations on the river, he meets an accountant in the colonial company. Marlow says that:

> I respected the fellow . . . His appearance was certainly that of a hairdresser's dummy; but in the great demoralization of the land he kept up his appearance. That's backbone. His starched collars and got-up shirt-fronts were achievements of character.[28]

The accountant shows a total lack of interest and compassion with regard to the people who suffer and die at the station, and he concentrates on the meticulous keeping of the books. The simplest way for a reader to treat this is as an irony on Marlow's part. Irony does not change a word in the text, but it turns the meaning around 180 degrees. However, the reasons for Marlow's praise may take us to many other aspects of the text, and involve Marlow's attitude to language and the notion of 'restraint'. If your interpretation of *Heart of Darkness* suggests that Marlow admires restraint above most other qualities, and that the importance of restraint is perhaps what the work is about, then this admiration may be interpreted as not being ironic, but highly serious.[29]

This example shows that the meaning of a single segment, or element, of a literary work can be given a completely different significance, depending on what the interpreter sees as the theme of the work; what the work is about. Here the conception of the whole, prior to finishing the work, guides the reader in identifying and assigning significance to elements within it. On the other hand, just one such element may also cause readers to change their conception of the theme. This example may therefore illustrate both Olsen's model of literary interpretation, and Gadamer's philosophical hermeneutics. If we combine Olsen's perspective with the fundamental role of Gadamer's hermeneutics, we see that readers are living humans being with a whole life guiding their gaze into the text – to put it a little floridly. To think that readers should attempt to keep their concerns and conceptions out of the encounter with the literary work is a widely held view, but to think that this goes without saying is naïve. The culture in which we live, the language whose concepts and categories we use, will all play a part in the process of understanding a work of literature. Also concerns more particular to the individual will be important. These will be active in our reading of the text, and also be activated by it.

We have seen above that Gadamer conceives of the reading of a work as a conversation about a subject matter, the truth about which reader and text share an interest. This common ground is one of the regulating features of the reading process according to Gadamer. This works well in the case of philosophical works, such as Aristotle's *Nicomachean Ethics*. The subject matter, what it is about, is shared by text and reader. This is not so clear, however, when it comes to literary works.[30] If we consider our example of *Heart of Darkness*, we see that the reading of the work, on the model we have discussed, is in great part to establish what it is about. Some well-known answers are that it is about the colonial exploitation of an African people, or that the journey is really the metaphorical journey into the European mind. Thus, the subject matter cannot so easily be an idea regulating the possible parameters of its interpretation, but the interpretation is at least in part the establishing of a subject matter.

What informs this view is the hermeneutic importance of the fact that interpretation is always application: that the knowledge or understanding you gain is a result both of a questioning of the text, and also an application of the work to your own situation. Knowledge may be general in character, but it is in the application to your own situation that it gets actualised and thus of interest to yourself, a self which is active in its relation to the world and its life. This puts a premium on works which are 'open', and there is no doubt a great deal of variation from one work to the other as to how open they are or can be, but the 'classical' works, the works of the canon, tend to be open to several themes, something our short performance history of *The Tempest* also showed. This means that there are several answers to what their subject matters are. However, much has now been made out of the openness of the work, but it is still only the sound of one hand clapping. Some resistance from the text is needed, and resistance can come in the form of the ability of literary works to tear the reader out of entrenched ways of understanding. The philosopher Bernard Harrison wrote a book called *Inconvenient Fictions*[31] where he argued that literary fictions test our preconceptions against a detailed and complex representation of human actions and perspectives. Harrison claims that it is literary theory, and not the literary works, which tempts us into a closed ideological vision. Clearly, the motivation of any reader must be to encounter something different from his or her own mental content when reading. The very act of attending to written material not your own must indicate a preparedness to be addressed by the text.

Perhaps the process of interpreting a literary work, where one's own interests must be weighed against the resistance of the work and its surprises, is also a training of one's mental as well as emotional capacities? Literature provides an arena for the application of terms, moral as well as cognitive, in the encounter with imaginary situations and characters. In making sense of a literary work one has to identify elements of it as more important than others, provide these with descriptions and redescriptions, and reach a view of what the literary work is about. In this process the meeting of the subjective element of one's own concerns and preoccupations and the objective existence of the text must be crucial, and the balancing between them must be on an at once cognitive and emotional plane. The process described clearly has elements of play, and playing is important. It is in play that children act out and try new roles and situations, and is therefore possibly one of the most productive activities in early life. As a species, *Homo sapiens* has a very long childhood, which allows us to develop further mentally and emotionally than other species. Literature may well be an extension of this into adult life, and this may add to its cognitive value.

In this chapter I have gone from 'what literary interpretation is' to 'what literary interpretation can be', and tied this latter feature to a recommended value which makes literature as a cultural phenomenon something special. I have also suggested possible ways of reading on this model which do give not only interpretation as a finished product a value, but which also gives the process a status of its own. This status is tied to the cognitive and experiential value which may be inherent in the process, where central concepts and principles of our lives meet the resistance of the text, and are developed further in interpretation.

FURTHER READING

A good introduction to the performance history of *The Tempest* is the editor's introduction to William Shakespeare, *The Tempest*, Stephen Orgel (ed.) (Oxford: Oxford University Press, 1987), pp. 1–87.

There are many introductions to Gadamer and hermeneutics. One of the better is the editor's introduction to Gadamer's *Philosophical Hermeneutics*, David E. Linge (ed. and trans.) (Berkeley, CA: University of California Press, 1976), pp. xi–lviii. A full length study is Georgia Warnke, *Gadamer: Hermeneutics, Tradition and Reason* (Cambridge: Polity, 1987).

Frank Kermode's *The Genesis of Secrecy: On the Interpretation of Narrative* (Cambridge, MA: Harvard University Press, 1979) is a highly interesting inquiry into the art of interpretation from an outstanding scholar and critic. The main texts he uses are the Gospels, and he brings to them an acquaintance both with traditional biblical scholarship and recent narrative theory, using these to ask fundamental questions about the motivation and aims of the interpretation of narratives.

NOTES

1. See Frank Kermode, *The Genesis of Secrecy: On the Interpretation of Narrative* (Cambridge, MA: Harvard University Press, 1979), pp. 81–2. See also *The Bible as Literature: An Introduction*, by John B. Gabel and Charles B. Wheeler (New York: Oxford University Press, 1986), p. 201.

2. I use 'producer' about the person who decides interpretation, and not 'director'. The American and the British usages are rather different, and usage differs also between film and theatre. In this case I side with the usage of the theatre and the British.

3. David Ward, ' "Now I will believe there are unicorns": *The Tempest* and its Theatre', *English*, 36 (1987), pp. 95–110 (p. 105).

4. This is an important difference from film and video, where one can go back and forth in the work. The same is true of taped theatrical performances, of course.

5. The application of the term 'openness' to literary works owes a debt to Umberto Eco and his text *The Open Work*, trans. Anna Cancogeni (London: Hutchinson Radius, 1989). This translation includes chapters from, among other works, *Opera Aperta* (Open Work), first published in Italian in 1962.

6. Jonathan Miller, in Ralph Berry (ed.) *On Directing Shakespeare* (London: Croom Helm, 1970), p. 39.

7. Miller in Berry, p. 40.

8. Davenant, Sir William, and John Dryden, 'The Tempest, or, The Enchanted Island: A Comedy', in Maximillian E. Novak (ed.), *The Works of*

John Dryden, vol. 10, textual ed. Robert Guffey (Berkeley, CA: University of California Press, 1970), pp. 1–103.

9. Charles Beecher Hogan, *Shakespeare in the Theatre 1701–1800: A Record of Performances in London 1701–1750* (Oxford: Clarendon, 1952), p. 460.

10. Daniel Wilson, *Caliban: The Missing Link* (London: Macmillan, 1873).

11. Wilson, pp. xi–xii.

12. Wilson, p. 73.

13. Mary M. Nilan, '*The Tempest* at the Turn of the Century: Cross-Currents in Production', *Shakespeare Survey*, 25 (1972), pp. 113–23 (p. 115).

14. Based on S. Belhassen's interview with Césaire in S. Belhassen, 'Aimé Césaire's A Tempest', in Lee Baxandall (ed.), *Radical Perspectives in the Arts* (Harmondsworth: Penguin, 1972), pp. 175–7.

15. See Kermode, *The Genesis of Secrecy*, chapter 1.

16. Hans-Georg Gadamer, *Truth and Method*, John Cumming and Garrett Barden (eds), trans. William Glen-Doepel, from the 2nd German edn (1965) of *Wahrheit und Methode*, 2nd English edn (London: Sheed and Ward, 1979).

17. Martin Heidegger, *Being and Time*, trans. John Macquarrie and Edward Robinson (Oxford: Blackwell, 1962).

18. Gadamer, *Truth and Method*, p. 236.

19. Gadamer, *Truth and Method*, p. 290.

20. Gadamer, *Truth and Method*, p. 297.

21. One philosopher has elaborated this model in a book. See Stein Haugom Olsen, *The Structure of Literary Understanding* (Cambridge: Cambridge University Press, 1978), pp. 82–117.

22. Even though most of his examples are from the interpretation of texts.

23. See Chapter 4 in this book.

24. We can also read non-literary texts in a literary way. This could prove fruitless, but the archaeologist Philip R. Davies claims that the reading of the Old Testament as literature has revolutionised biblical archaeology. See Philip R. Davies, *In Search of 'Ancient Israel'*, *Journal for the Study of the Old Testament*, Supplement Series 148 (Sheffield: Sheffield Academic Press, 1992), pp. 11–21.

25. Stein Haugom Olsen, *The End of Literary Theory*, 'The "Meaning" of a Literary Work', pp. 53–72 (p. 56).

26. There is also an 'outer narrator', not named, who reports the story told by Marlow aboard a boat on the Thames.

27. The location is never given in the work, but everything indicates that this is the setting of the main action of the work.

28. Joseph Conrad, *Youth, Heart of Darkness, The End of the Tether*, Robert Kimbrough (ed.) (Oxford: Oxford University Press, 1984), p. 68.

29. I elaborate on this interpretation of *Heart of Darkness* in 'Restraint in the Darkness', *English Studies*, 76 (1995), pp. 52–63.

30. For a more thorough discussion of this problem with Gadamer's herme-
    neutics, see the second part of my 'Anachronistic Themes and Literary
    Value: *The Tempest*', *British Journal of Aesthetics*, 31 (1991), pp. 122–33.
31. Bernard Harrison, *Inconvenient Fictions: Literature and the Limits of Theory*
    (New Haven, CT: Yale University Press, 1991).

SIX

LITERATURE IN PHILOSOPHY?

The heading of this chapter might be a little misleading. It is true that a few works by philosophers are quite similar to literary works, and in fact some philosophers have written novels, plays and poems. However, this chapter is not about these works. The chapter is mainly about how philosophical texts can, and perhaps should, be read with the same degree of attention to form that we use when reading literary works. By that I mean not that we should expect the same of philosophy as we do of literature. Kant's *Critique of Pure Reason* is not going to be as exciting as Dostoevsky's *Crime and Punishment*, or at least not in the same way. Rather, the way the philosophical work is written, the choices of the author, the sometimes cunning ways in which the reader is influenced by the form of the writing is worth noticing. This chapter will address questions of how form influences philosophical content, and look at diverse examples.

In antiquity philosophy was developed, mainly by Plato, as the antithesis of rhetoric. Plato's early Socratic dialogues show this very well. Sophists,[1] the teachers and practitioners of rhetoric, the art of persuasion, were set up as the enemies of the disinterested search for truth. Philosophy, on the other hand, was conceived as precisely this disinterested search for truth. Plato argued that the sophists were just hired mouths, arguing whatever point they were paid for. Their technique of influencing minds through the use of words, rhetoric, was discredited. It worked best when not noticed, and was seen by Plato and others to be more in the way of an infection of the mind. Beliefs and emotions were planted in listeners without notice by cunning rhetoricians. The rational mind of auditors was bypassed by the tricks at the disposal of these skilled speakers (though Plato's Socrates doubted that they really had a skill). Plato put philosophy forward as the cure for this kind of infection. Philosophy would be the disinterested search for truth which worked through *activating* the rational mind of people, not bypassing it, and set up 'dialectic' as the way to achieve the lofty goals of rational endeavour.

Since Plato philosophy has looked askance at rhetoric, which is seen by many as cheating, since rhetoric aims at persuasion, not argumentation. But as the British philosopher Bernard Williams asks in *Shame and Necessity*: how could Plato hope to convince without persuasion? Philosophy 'should consist of dialogue and not monologue, that . . . is essentially *exchange*. But how could reason exchange anything without persuasion?'.[2] I think the answer is that it cannot. Argument is a way of persuasion, and few are those writers, even in philosophy, who do not try to persuade readers in ways other than just setting out a series of arguments. This comes in many forms, but philosophy has recently become an increasingly narrow kind of writing.

In the twentieth century, philosophy became very professionalised, and adopted the ways other academic subjects, notably the sciences, disseminate their ideas. The professional philosopher these days tries to find some time between teaching, supervision and administration to write a paper for a forthcoming conference. It is quite often done at the last minute. The presentation at the conference is usually met with a few critical questions from members of the audience, and then it is back to the drawing-board. After a few amendments the article is sent off to a refereed journals where other overworked academics judge whether it is worthy of publication. Once the academic has a few such articles published, the time has come to persuade a publisher to publish a book based on the articles and some others yet unpublished. I would hazard the guess that most philosophy books published in the English language these days have started in the way just outlined.

It is small wonder, then, that matters of style and attention to the art of writing tend to go by the board. The choices of format, presentation and style tend to be taken for you. If you want to get a job teaching philosophy, and to get ahead once you are on board, you have to stick to the stated and unstated norms. It is therefore unsurprising that philosophy since the mid twentieth century has shown decreasing signs of stylistic innovation, though there are exceptions such as Jaques Derrida and Stanley Cavell. In what follows I shall first present a way of thinking about form and style with reference to philosophy, and then go on to consider three examples from two different epochs in the history of philosophy. The terms 'form' and 'style' are sometimes used as synonyms, as we shall see when Berel Lang writes about the anatomy of philosophical style. I shall use 'form' to mean loosely the organising principles of a text, such as the 'genre' ('article', 'book', 'dialogue') and its structure, and 'style', equally loosely, to mean its manner of address. This can be formal, informal, condescending, inquisitive and so on. For our purposes, the main distinction is between the phenomena of style and form on the one hand, and content on the other. We saw in the introduction that the history of philosophy shows a wide range of styles and genres, whereas the present has few examples of such variety. This does not mean, however, that the style of recent philosophy is of no interest, and two of my examples are from the mid-twentieth century.

FORM, STYLE AND CONTENT: TWO MODELS
In the analysis of literature it is a truism that form influences content, yet form is most often ignored in the understanding of philosophical works. Is this because philosophy is so different from literature that form does not influence content, or is the form of philosophy so transparent that it cannot possibly influence the content of what is put forward? There are at least two parts to this issue. One is whether or not the writer has consciously considered form and style to be integral elements in the philosophy. The other is whether style and form may still influence the content, no matter what the writer's intention has been. As readers of philosophy we should consider the influence style and form may have on our understanding of the text, and if and how we are being influenced by it.

In *The Anatomy of Philosophical Style*[3] Berel Lang introduces the distinction between the 'neutralist' and the 'interactionist' models in the debate around form and content in philosophy. The 'neutralist' denies that the form or structure of philosophy has any connection with its substance, 'the relation is viewed as at most ornamental, at its least as accidental and irrelevant, even as a hindrance or occasion of philosophical obfuscation'.[4] For those who have a background in studies of literature, this position seems less than convincing, but there are clear advantages to a situation where this view is true. First, all philosophical works, be they Plato's dialogues, Wittgenstein's aphorisms, Pascal's 'thoughts' or Hume's treatise, can all be discussed on a common ground. Granted, their forms are different, but those forms can be dispensed with and we can discuss the simple propositions connecting subjects and predicates that are at the bottom of whatever forms are chosen by the authors. We can extract, then, a common linguistic core which can be placed in a uniform field of discourse. This would also help us to see similarities over time, to point to previous sources and influences, whereas the individual philosophers seem to stress, not least through their styles of writing, how different they are from all past philosophy. If this neutralist perspective is accepted, we can also entertain some hope of progress in philosophy. Given a common ground, philosophers may even be able to build on the achievements of the past, rather than 'reinvent the wheel', so to speak. This would be valuable, for we could even have some hope of progress in philosophy. That is, if this model were plausible. We know that it is certainly not applicable to all philosophy. If we start almost at the beginning, with Plato whom we discussed in Chapter 2, we see that he never put forward any propositions which could be identified clearly as his own. In a majority of dialogues it is Socrates who is the protagonist, and who puts forward and discusses issues. Is he speaking for Plato, and if we assume this, are there not times when this seems highly unlikely? If Socrates makes mistakes in elementary logic, are we not supposed to notice this and think that the author does not speak through him? That such questions can be asked shows us that texts may have to be reconstructed and, yes, interpreted in order to fit into a kind of common discourse of philosophy. In interpreting texts in this way, we have to make choices that are not innocent with regard to views and positions on philosophical questions. That is, two people with dissimilar views on philosophical issues may very well read different positions into the dialogues of Plato, to stay with the example we started with.

This brings us to the 'interactionist' model of philosophical discourse. According to this model, philosophers, by choosing a style or form for what they are putting forward, also choose content. Rather than content being like a fluid the philosopher can pour into any of a series of forms, as on the neutralist model, the content according to the interactionist model is at least in part shaped by the form chosen.

While the view expressed here is the orthodoxy in literary studies, it is far from uncontroversial in philosophy and carries with it a set of problems, some of which we shall look at here and now. Formal features of literary works do not, as such, pose problems. The narrative structure of Marlow's story as reported by an outside narrator in Conrad's *Heart of Darkness*, is a major feature of the work. Without it, it would definitely not be the same work. But literary works are supposed to be unique, to stand alone, and to be read for pleasure or their aesthetic value. Works of philosophy, by contrast, are supposed to contribute to an ongoing debate about the deep questions of human existence. They are expected either to refute previous suggestions to the age-old problems of philosophy or to offer new solutions, preferably both. The expectation is that they contribute to a continuing discussion, and that they should offer themselves up for this kind of treatment. To take issue with a view or position, you may have to identify that position, probably in your own words. To offer your criticism or alternative solution to problems discussed or presented, you will have to be in the same conceptual field.

One reason why it is difficult to see novels, poems or plays to be works of philosophy is that they do not operate on the same conceptual level as philosophy. If the novel is any good, for instance, it will not be a treatise offering arguments. It is more likely to be a good story, but maybe you will see that the themes of the novel, what it is about, connect with problems that are also the concern of philosophy. However, this line of thinking may be too categorical in that it does not take account of the matter of degrees. Some kinds of writing, and their effects, may be closely tied to their form. This would be the case with poems, for instance. Few poems survive being 'translated' into prose, but this may not apply only to poetry. The aphoristic style of the philosopher Ludwig Wittgenstein also seems to resist translation into other styles, as we shall see later in this chapter. Both Wittgenstein and Plato are philosophers who have written in styles not widely adopted in philosophy. Hardly any of their followers, who have been willing to call themselves either Platonists or Wittgenstinians, have written in the same styles as their masters. Rather, they have argued in more or less plain prose what their masters would have said had they written theses, and have supplied supporting arguments to these positions and fended off criticisms from others. So the exchanges and discussions that many see as the life-blood of philosophy are conducted in a different stylistic landscape, so to speak, than the pronouncements (if such they are) of two of the most influential philosophers of all time.

Style and form contribute to the effect and maybe even the content of philosophy, but do not make it impossible to interact with philosophy in different styles. Style may not be a barrier to communication, but it does pose difficulties. How important style and form are to the effect and content of philosophy cannot be discussed in isolation from concrete examples, so discussing concrete examples is just what we are going to do, and we are going to start at the beginning, with Plato. We saw in Chapter 2 that Plato was among the first, at least on record, to have thought of himself as a philosopher. In fact, he is often seen as 'inventing' philosophy as an undertaking separate from others. Yet we have nothing from his hand where he speaks in his own voice, unless we count some letters, several of which are of dubious provenance. The question of point of view is, as in literary works, also a matter of interpretation. Philosophers know that Plato was highly influenced by Socrates, and it is very tempting to take what Socrates says in the dialogues as the views of the author, Plato. Even Jaques Derrida seems to do this in his widely discussed work on

Plato's *Phaedrus*, 'Plato's Pharmacy'.[5] In Chapter 4 we briefly outlined and discussed deconstruction, which is inspired by Derrida, and we saw that it is a kind of deep-seated scepticism based on the fluid nature of language. Part of the strategy of deconstruction is to subject terms of opposition where one dominates the other, such as literature/philosophy, writing/speech and absence/presence, to pressure and to show that these can be reversed or exploded. The result, apparently, is then a completely new conceptual landscape. One such opposition is between writing and speech, and since Plato to many is the founding figure of western philosophy, Socrates' criticism of writing in *Phaedrus* is a defining moment in western philosophy. Part of Derrida's strategy here is to show that the order of priority of this opposition can be reversed through exhibiting indeterminacies in Plato's writing, for instance that when he refers to writing as a *pharmakon*, this Greek word can be translated both as 'poison' and 'remedy'. However, Derrida's reading of this dialogue is not particularly sophisticated, as shown by Gianni Ferrari's discussion.[6] He also seems to assume that Plato does nothing to remedy the faults of writing listed by Socrates in the writing of his own dialogue. But this need not necessarily be the case, as we are going to see exemplified when Socrates overlooks the qualities of Lysias' speech in the dialogue we are about to examine more closely.

ADVERTISING PHILOSOPHY: PLATO AND THE *PHAEDRUS*[7]

The dialogue *Phaedrus*[8] was probably written at the end of Plato's so-called 'middle' period, or even at the beginning of his 'late' period. We do not know for sure, and the dating is mainly a matter of interpretation. One of the matters to consider when trying to date a dialogue of Plato is if there are new ideas introduced which have not occurred in some dialogues, but which do occur in others. Another matter is style. We believe that Plato's style changed with time, and that dialogues which were written early were 'aporetic', which means that they end without having come to any sort of conclusion. *Hippias Major*, which we discussed in Chapter 3, is one of these. Also, with the notable exception of *Philebus*, Plato did not use Socrates as his main character in the later dialogues.

What interests us in the context of 'literature in philosophy' is how this Platonic dialogue shows how style and form influence and contribute to its philosophical content. The dialogue is about the competing claims of philosophy and of rhetoric over the allegiance of a young and impressionable man, Phaedrus. The themes of the dialogue are inextricably interwoven with its structure and style, to the degree that it is difficult to maintain the distinction between form and content. In the prologue to his book on Plato's *Sophist*,[9] Stanley Rosen distinguishes between two approaches to studying Plato which he calls the ontological and the dramatic, and these correspond more or less to Lang's 'neutralist' and 'interactionist', only here with two distinct kinds of actual approaches to the study of Plato's works in mind. In Chapter 2 our approach to *Ion* and book 10 of the *Republic* was mainly ontological, in Rosen's terminology. Our purpose was to discover what Plato, through Socrates, said about the relationship between philosophy and literature. We focused on parts of the texts, without paying much attention to the dialogues as organic wholes. Here, with *Phaedrus*, we are going to adopt the dramatic approach, to regard:

> the dialogue as a unity, and more specifically, as a work of art in which the natures of the speakers, as well as the circumstances under which they converse, all play a part in the doctrine or philosophical significance of the text.[10]

The dialogue is much too rich for us to be able to cover more than some aspects of it, unfortunately,[11] but first a summary of what happens in the dialogue. Socrates, who is a mature man, meets the young Phaedrus one day outside the city of Athens. While there he clearly intends to practise reading a speech by the sophist Lysias. Socrates guesses that Phaedrus has learnt the speech by heart, but gets him to read the speech to him. The speech is supposed to be by a man who feigns not to be in love with a boy, and who argues for the benefits of a sexual relationship between them which is not based on love. This speech must be seen in the context of the conventionally condoned relationships in Greece at the time between a younger boy and an older man, where the older man gave guidance and support to the younger man in return for sexual favours.[12] Socrates is not impressed by this speech, and Phaedrus forces him to make another speech based on the same premise. To do this, Socrates veils his face (in shame, we assume). The speech differs from Lysias' in many ways, including that it starts with a definition. When this speech is over, Socrates finds that he has to make amends for his insult to the god Eros, for he has spoken falsely about this god. He makes his amends by a new speech, which begins by a recantation of his first. The core of the speech takes the form of a mythical allegory about the nature of the soul. It has to be an allegory because 'what manner of thing it is would be a long tale to tell, and most assuredly a God alone could tell it; but what it resembles, that a man might tell in briefer compass' (246a). The soul is likened to a charioteer with two winged steeds, one 'good' the other 'bad'.

Together these get to see glimpses of the area above the heavens where the forms reside, but they acquire bodies and forget what they saw. However, through the recollection of beauty itself – the form of beauty brought about by seeing beauty in the beautiful boy, they may also regain knowledge of the other ideas. So, the relationship between boy and man, beloved and lover, is the basis for a philosophical life. Thus, the second speech is also relevant for the relationship between Phaedrus and Socrates, and perhaps between the dialogue and readers.

After his second speech, Socrates prays that Lysias, whose theory was false, may turn to philosophy, and also that his follower Phaedrus may be converted to the philosophical way of life. He also adds that his speech 'was perforce poetical, to please Phaedrus'. In the latter part of the dialogue they debate rhetoric, how to speak and write well. One of the topics is whether or not the speaker has to know the subject well, or whether it is enough to seem to know it. Socrates is a strong advocate of having knowledge of the subject, and how to fashion one's utterances to address different publics. Their discussion over, they unite in prayer and depart.

So, the first half of the dialogue consists mainly of the practice of rhetoric, the performance of speeches, while the latter concerns the theory of rhetoric. There are, however, several themes of the dialogue, and its own skill of addressing its own public is one of them, and one we shall come back to shortly.

There is no outside narrator in the *Phaedrus*, and the two interlocutors are left to introduce themselves. This feature is more like modern drama, involving the reader more directly in what is going on, and readers have to make up their own minds about the characters. When the dialogue begins, Socrates spots Phaedrus outside the city walls and hails him with two of the most innocent, and at the same time most philosophical, questions there are: 'Where do you come from, Phaedrus my friend, and where are you going?' (227a). This sentence is clearly an opening which should lead a philosophically inclined reader to know in what frame of mind to read the dialogue. While it is too simple to say that Socrates represents philosophy and Phaedrus rhetoric, the personalities of the two are indeed different. Phaedrus comes across as an enthusiast, he lives, not, it appears, to understand the issues deeper, or to reach a true and settled opinion on a matter, but to hear and perform speeches and to organise discussions. For him the quantity is more important than the quality, and he can be seen to operate almost like an impresario. His attitude represents a challenge which Socrates cannot pass up, so Socrates must think that Phaedrus may be 'converted' to philosophy, to the search for firm knowledge rather than what seems likely. Socrates, on his part, emphasises his own oddity. He walks around barefoot, as he always does, and when Phaedrus chooses a very appropriate site where to sit and talk, the very appropriateness is highly acclaimed by Socrates. He breaks out into florid prose to bring out all the advantages of the location, and we imagine Phaedrus shaking his head in disbelief. But this has thematic importance. Phaedrus is an intellectual impresario, valuing the effects of wisdom above wisdom itself, and it is this aspect of his personality that Socrates highlights with his praise.

Thus, the two partners in conversation introduce themselves. And Plato, who himself is as absent as in his other dialogues, thus makes Phaedrus appear not to be his own man, but a mouthpiece for another person who is absent, Lysias. These are aspects that influence any reader's views of the respective credibility the two characters, and they are not reducible to the statements of the characters. Plato did not write theses or conference papers, but rather dialogues which in appearance are quite like one of the literary genres of today, the play. To ignore the genre in assessing the philosophy expounded in the *Phaedrus* is very risky. Also, we must remember that Plato wrote at a time when philosophy was not even properly established. The whole approach of philosophy, the methodical search for truth, was not established or known outside of a very small circle. To gain wider currency for philosophy, it was necessary to address a wider public in a form this public could relate to.

As we just saw, when taking their place under the tree, Socrates also brings in the background to their conversation. One reason for this is to highlight Phaedrus' personality, but this is not the only occasion when the background is not allowed to stay in the background. That the setting becomes a theme of the work this early highlight both the importance of the medium and the organisation of the setting. It also indicates that writing – far from necessarily just drifting all over the place – can engineer its own intellectual setting (and hence its reception) to a certain extent: writing can be made easy or difficult, cloaked or naked – and may also draw attention to itself. Just as Socrates has explicitly drawn attention to the physical setting of the conversation beside the Ilissus.

When Socrates draws attention to the cicadas singing in the background, at the transition from the first part of the dialogue to the second (258e–259d) (a caution not to let attention slip), it is another instance of the same ploy: the background is not left alone, but brought into play. The relevance for the criticism of writing, which we are going to look at soon, is clear: background and medium have common features. Both are usually taken for granted since they are the prism through which the content is to be seen clearly, and in most cases they are most effective when not noticed. Hence, by drawing attention to the background, and thus switching the background into the foreground of discussion, Plato also prepares his readers for the criticism of writing. In the case of the latter we shall also see a reversal: what is taken for granted, the medium of the communication, suddenly becomes part of the communication itself. The criticism of writing therefore comes as the last element in a cumulative chain of reversals, and the jolting effect of any of these elements is surely not incidental. These patterns are not instances of audience manipulation along the lines of the prevalent rhetoricians of the day, but attempts on the part of Plato to utilise the medium of the dialogue in the service of his conception of philosophy in that readers are not provoked into *specific* responses, but rather to initiate reflective *processes*. The attentive reader is provoked to launch an inquiry into the possible reasons for these odd structured transitions within the dialogue.

Let us look at what the dialogue's criticism of writing consists in. In the second part, Socrates claims that writing is close to useless, since a piece of writing once written down can only say the same thing over and over (275d4–9). Yet while fixed in this sense, it is extremely fluid in another; for a script will circulate indiscriminately among all audiences, incapable of selecting those who can receive it with understanding (275d9–e5). A living speaker, by contrast, and especially the philosophic discussant, can choose an appropriate conversational partner, can answer when questioned and so can expect to sow the seeds of fresh speech in the soul of the hearer (276e4–7a4).[13]

By having Phaedrus 'stand in' for Lysias in the early part of the dialogue, Plato not only presents arguments for this position through the character Socrates, he also displays the dangers he warns of. For this to hold water, however, Lysias must be misrepresented by Phaedrus and misunderstood by Socrates. I think this can be shown to be the case since Lysias' speech is much better written and conceived than either Socrates, and gradually also Phaedrus, would have it. Socrates also says that 'Lysias is here among us' (228e), but he is *not* present to defend himself. The point is that his writing is misunderstood by Socrates and Phaedrus, but we, as readers, will not necessarily misunderstand it. We can see that it has merits beyond those that Socrates seems to notice, chiefly through its form and style being so relaxed as to make its content (that the young boy should, in effect, act as a prostitute) appear much less outrageous. For us, the very presence of the criticism of writing in this dialogue will make us ask of the speech by Lysias actually present in the dialogue, whether it falls foul of the shortcomings Socrates draws our attention to, and thus the reader is activated in relation not only to the speech by Lysias, but also the dialogue as a whole. This makes us see that Socrates fails to understand Lysias' text, and we are inclined to defend it against him. Hence, the shortcoming of writing that Socrates alerts us to makes us enter into a dialogue with the text, and thus breaking the restrictions on its usefulness that Socrates has introduced. This further demonstrates the kind of process Plato may have wanted to initiate with regard to his own text, and this, in turn, would require that Socrates is not the mouthpiece of Plato.

This is not the only way the criticism of writing is important for the understanding of the dialogue. This theme is a key to how the dialogue selects the audience appropriate to itself: those philosophically sophisticated enough to pursue the apparent inconsistency and its implications for the rest of the dialogue are 'those who understand it' rather than those who 'have no business with it'. The dialogue is freed from the dangers of writing emphasised in 275e since only those who read it thoroughly and ask the relevant philosophical questions of the text will read it as philosophy. Thus, it might be said, the *Phaedrus* selects the audience appropriate for itself through the criticism of its own medium.[14] We therefore see that this written dialogue is like the speaker in 276e4–7a4, and can select its own audience, can 'answer' when questioned, and has indeed sown the seeds both of fresh speech and fresh writing in the souls of readers. With regard to Derrida's 'Plato's Pharmacy', we see that Derrida's supposed fixed opposition between speech and writing is quite consciously not there in the *Phaedrus*, since both speech and writing share the same benefits and drawbacks, and that Plato's writing of this dialogue is much more elaborate and sophisticated than Derrida allows for.

We have seen, in this discussion of some aspects of this rich and entertaining dialogue, that the 'dramatic' reading of it yields results that have philosophical implications. It is precisely the 'dramatic' form of the dialogue which is the key to how it is supposed to communicate with its readers, and activate their 'philosophical natures' despite Socrates' warnings about the dangers of writing. Further, it is an important element of the work that the two discussion partners are depicted in the way that they are. In many ways it is Socrates the philosopher who, in regard to Phaedrus, has much the same position as Plato the philosopher has in regard to the readers of the dialogue. One theme in the dialogue is persuasion, how to make people change the way they act and think. This is what Socrates tries to achieve in his dealing with Phaedrus. In their exchanges this comes up in the relationship between the lover and the beloved, but this also reflects on the relationship between themselves. In their case, philosophy as the search for truth is equated with the love between the lover and the beloved. How to discover and foster this disposition in another soul is really what Socrates is concerned to discuss, and in relation to this the persuasion of others through the use of language.

If we step outside the frame of the dialogue, the same question comes up in our reading of the dialogue. How can Plato, who never utters a word in his own voice, persuade readers of his views? It is possible that for Plato his own answers to philosophical questions are secondary in importance to turning people to the search for truth. As we saw in the second chapter, philosophy was a new discourse which had to compete with established and traditional ways of answering the deepest questions. In this dialogue, Plato has used the literary means at his disposal to activate the critical faculties of his readers. He writes entertainingly and beautifully, all in order to convert readers to the painstaking search for truth which is the philosophical way of life. It is arguable that in the competition between literature and philosophy which Plato sets up in the *Ion* and the *Republic*, he uses the weapons of the opposition to further his own cause in the *Phaedrus*.

We can, as we have tried here, untangle the webs of form and content, and point to how the structure and the dramatic effects are designed to influence and activate readers. None of these effects and influences can be active once they have been 'translated' into more or less plain prose. The body of the work is no longer alive when we do this, so to speak, and our activity takes more or less the form of an autopsy. However, it seems possible to effect this translation, to look at how it works, and then to return to the work and find it still alive.

We have to remind ourselves that the *Phaedrus* was one of the first self-consciously philosophical works, and yet we find it surprisingly modern. Its form is dramatic, and consists only of the utterances of the two characters. Few other philosophers have used dialogue as their medium, and fewer still have succeeded. We shall now turn to a philosopher whose writings are not dramatic, and do not consist of dialogue. His writings are definitely modern, and have been even less emulated.

TWO STYLES: WITTGENSTEIN

The Austrian philosopher Ludwig Wittgenstein, quite possibly the most influential philosopher of the twentieth century, wrote in an inimitable style, or perhaps two styles. However, this does not mean that we cannot appropriate his philosophy. Wittgenstein's philosophy is subject to several different interpretations based, often, on differing emphases.

Some focus on his background in mathematics and logic, some on the cultural and aesthetic influences from his native Vienna, others again on 'the text only'. All, however, assume that it is possible to 'translate' his writings into a form which can interact with other styles of philosophy. This implies that it is possible to say what Wittgenstein 'means' – one is not forced to do so in the same style. However, it is also a moot point whether or not 'something' goes missing in such translations from one style to the other. In the case of Wittgenstein this is certainly so, and the artistry of his writing is only the most obvious casualty. Another point worth considering, but perhaps difficult to answer, is whether Wittgenstein would have had the same impact on philosophy in the past century if he had written in the same style as most other philosophers. Indeed, if he even *could* have written what he wanted to express in their style.

In his first work, the only one to be published in his lifetime, Wittgenstein sought to establish the relationship between language and world, what can be said and thought, and what cannot. This is difficult enough, and Wittgenstein felt that very few people, if any, understood either his attempts to prove this relationship, or the relationship itself, and maybe the style is to blame? Let us look at his style in the famous first lines of *Tractatus Logico-Philosophicus:*[15]

1	The world is all that is the case.
1.1	The world is the totality of facts, not of things.
1.11	The world is determined by the facts, and by their being *all* the facts.
1.12	For the totality of facts determines what is the case, and also whatever is not the case.
1.13	The facts in logical space are the world.
1.2	The world divides into facts.
1.21	Each item can be the case or not the case while everything else remains the same.
2	What is the case – a fact – is the existence of states of affairs.[16]

These sentences are not arguments; they are statements, where each decimal numbered paragraph is a commentary on preceding ones.[17] When the *Tractatus* was finished, Wittgenstein claimed that he had solved the problems of philosophy, and turned to other activities. Reading it, it clearly shows, through its form, that it is meant to be the final word on the basic problems of philosophy. The statements are very definite and beautifully written, but according to Wittgenstein himself very few did or even could understand them. However, Wittgenstein returned to philosophy some eight years after the first publication of the *Tractatus*, both because he felt misunderstood and because he came to see that the problems he thought he had solved were not the real problems of philosophy. In order to get a position at Cambridge, he was awarded a Ph.D. on the basis of the *Tractatus*, published eight years earlier. One may wonder whether a work in this style could be accepted as a Ph.D. today.

When Wittgenstein started to write again, his style was still very much his own, but it had changed substantially. In *Philosophical Investigations*,[18] published posthumously, Wittgenstein's view of philosophy and its problems had changed, and this change is also reflected in his style. Rather than giving an account of how language mirrors reality as in the *Tractatus*, the *Investigations* tries to show how philosophical problems arise out of our misconceptions of how language works. He called it an album, he found it impossible to write it from beginning to end, and it appears as a series of 'snapshots' or loose sketches, even if series of paragraphs are devoted to the same line of inquiry.[19] The paragraphs are no longer mainly short statements, but have a lot more examples and questions since he wanted to remind us how language is connected with reality. He wants to make us conscious of what is really innate or tacit knowledge, and shows us how we use certain words and concepts in a wealth of everyday, artistic and scientific contexts. Take this first half of a paragraph from the *Investigations*:

> 139. When someone says the word 'cube' to me, for example, I know what it means. But can the whole *use* of the word come before my mind, when I *understand* it in this way?
>
> Well, but on the other hand isn't the meaning of the word also determined by its use? And can these ways of determining meaning conflict? Can what we grasp *in a flash* accord with a use, fit or fail to fit it? And how can what is present to us in an instant, what comes before our mind in an instant, fit a *use*? . . .

This example is not untypical of the style of this work. It is quite clear that it would have been impossible for Wittgenstein to have written this latter work in the style of the former, and neither would he have been able to write it in the style or form of the scientific paper. It is a fundamental belief in his later philosophy that the activity of philosophy 'is a battle against the bewitchment of our intelligence by means of language',[20] and in order to effect this cure the way philosophy is presented must activate the critical faculties of the reader. He even tries to slow down the reading of his work through the use of punctuation marks.[21]

If we try to imagine the later phase in Wittgenstein's philosophy written in the style of the former, we find that its inquisitive probing of issues and the extensive use of examples would not at all fit in with the polished and beautiful statements of the *Tractatus*. The very nature of Wittgenstein's later philosophy is to show differences and to question the settled ways our minds work, and to make us see our world anew. This purpose would not be well served by the style of the *Tractatus*. The case of Wittgenstein, therefore, shows the different styles of the two phases of his philosophy to be intimately linked with the differences in philosophical approach, and seem to support the interactionist model. As with Plato, the style of writing is intimately connected with the content of the philosophy. While Wittgenstein did not have to 'invent' philosophy, he did have to invent his own style in order to convey both the radical nature of his proposals and, in the case of his later philosophy, the diverse ways in which language can constitute our activities.

It may be argued that Wittgenstein's impact has been weakened by his style as well. The mass of commentary on Wittgenstein, however, has a form and a purpose very different from those of the master. Very few of his followers have adopted his fresh style and approach to philosophy. They have mainly been concerned with explaining his philosophy and defending it against misunderstandings, some also with taking his insights into fields of inquiry where Wittgenstein himself did not venture, all, however, in the commonly accepted norms of style and form in modern philosophy. It is arguable that both Plato and Wittgenstein are the odd ones out in philosophy, and that their respective styles are inimitable and atypical. The same cannot be said of Quine, who does indeed write according to the commonly accepted norms of today, only better than most.

TAKING EMPIRICISM METAPHORICALLY: QUINE

Unlike Plato, Willard van Orman Quine, born in 1908, had the benefit of writing at a time when philosophy was well established, and when people were generally literate. He was one of the most prominent representatives of analytic philosophy in the latter half of the twentieth century, and a Professor at possibly America's most prestigious university, Harvard. He started his academic career as a mathematician, and gradually turned to logic. His first notable contributions were in this field, but his range widened to include ontology and epistemology. In his autobiography, *The Time of My Life*,[22] he reveals that at some point in his early twenties he vacillated between becoming an author or a mathematician. He could not be both, he felt. We know the result, but it may be said that he fulfilled both ambitions, at least in the sense that his writings are exceptionally well written. Philosophical writings in the fields where Quine excelled are not generally considered to have any literary merit, but Quine manages to make it all engaging. It would be to go too far to say that his books and articles are 'page-turners', but they certainly manage to keep the interest of the reader.

Quine's philosophical views are associated with 'hard' movements such as logical empiricism and behaviourism. The latter view seeks to dispense with mentalistic concepts in psychology and the philosophy of mind. Mentalistic concepts are those which are 'from within', i.e. which are irreducibly those of the first-person perspective, and which cannot be checked against observable criteria. Behaviourists do not necessarily deny that there is an inner perspective in these fields, but deem that they are not scientifically acceptable. Together with his uncompromising views in other philosophical debates, Quine has been seen as the most prominent representative of 'hard' analytic philosophy, where the 'job' of philosophy is to be 'the handmaiden of science', a position which implies that philosophy is the most general and abstract field of science. It is clear that this is a view which is not favourable to the linking of literature to philosophy, and it is therefore of particular interest to see if and how we can use the insights of literary studies to understand the way Quine communicates his views.

'Two Dogmas of Empiricism' is one of the most celebrated pieces of philosophy in the twentieth century. It was published in *Philosophical Review* in 1951, and again in the collection *From a Logical Point of View*.[23] The first dogma he argues against is the commonly accepted view that there are two kinds of truth, those that can be verified with reference to the world, synthetic truths, and analytic truths, which can be verified with reference only to the norms of the language. The time-honoured example of this latter kind of statement is 'bachelors are unmarried men'. This distinction is often attributed to Kant. The second dogma is reductionism, 'the belief that each meaningful statement is equivalent to some logical construct upon terms which refer to immediate experience'.[24] Quine wants to get rid of these dogmas in order to be more thoroughgoing in his empiricism, and claims that Kant's account of the semantics of analyticity – that the predicate is contained in the subject – is just a metaphorical notion.[25]

Still, Quine's own alternative, sketched on the last few pages of the article, is even more metaphorical. A powerful picture is drawn up where knowledge is likened with a network – or a field of force.[26] The interior of this web is theory, whereas the outer reaches are based on observation-statements. The fault of most empiricists is that they have considered all our knowledge to be directly affirmable by observation, whereas there are any number of ways awkward evidence, at the edge of the web, can be accommodated by effecting changes closer to the centre of the web of knowledge or belief. For instance, the most effective way of brushing off evidence which conflicts with the existing web of belief, is to attribute this evidence to hallucination. However, this is also the most radical solution since it opens up the possibility that the existing system of beliefs is also based on a similarly untrustworthy basis.

The inner core of this web of belief is connected to most of the outer reaches, to continue within the metaphor, and this is the reason we are loath to change our logic, for instance, or our basic theoretical glue such as causality. Any changes in the centre would have large-scale effects on the whole system of thought, changes at the centre are just too 'costly' in terms of the changes we would have to make. These claims aside, what we are interested in here is to see how the philosopher who dismisses Kant's account of analyticity as just 'metaphor' fares with his own use of language. Is his own alternative any less metaphorical?

It would appear not. Some reasons are presented already, but let us have a closer look at what Quine writes. His own suggestions come at the end of the article, and are the most interesting in terms of form and style. We have seen already that Quine thinks that the distinction between analytic and synthetic statements is untenable, and we have also seen the general outlines of his own preferred model. What interests us now is not the content of his suggestions, but how they are written.

With his quip that 'our statements about the external world face the tribunal of sense experience not individually but only as a corporate body',[27] Quine introduces his own alternative. It is a powerful picture, but is hardly any less metaphorical than Kant's account of analyticity. Quine realises this, and writes that he has for the sake of vividness spoken about distance from a sensory periphery, based on the picture we are already familiar with, the picture of the web of belief. And now he wants to 'clarify this notion without metaphor'.[28] However, within the second sentence after this wish, he is back within the picture of the web of belief, and he stays there. He talks about the 'location' of this or that kind of statement, the 'centrality' or the 'peripheral nature' of this or that phenomenon, all with reference to the web of belief.

My account is not done with the objective of suggesting that Quine did not see what he was doing, that he was blind to his own language, or that there was a discrepancy between what he wanted to write and the way he wrote it. That the writer was blind, but that I can see. Derrida, in 'White Mythology',[29] argues that the distinction between the literal, or proper, and the metaphorical is essential to the constitution of philosophy, and requires the privileging of the former. This distinction is itself drawn within philosophy, but remains metaphorical. This realisation leads to an explosion of this opposition, and 'metaphor, then, always carries its death within itself. And this death, surely, is also the death *of* philosophy'.[30] As with the opposition between speech and writing we have discussed above, this explosion fails to make much noise once one realises that the opposition it poses is false. Clearly, philosophy cannot but be metaphorical, as most uses of language are. The quotation from Doris Lessing in Chapter 1 brings out the reliance on metaphor even when scientists communicate their cosmology and sub-atomic physics, and Plato in writing the *Phaedrus* was clearly aware of it. Even if Quine seems to wish his own metaphors away, any distinction between philosophy and literature cannot rely on the blind worship of clean and tidy oppositions.[31]

So, the present analysis is not a deconstruction. What we are interested in is to see how the author uses the means at his disposal to persuade the readers that his account of the relationship between beliefs and evidence is better than the one based on the distinction between analytic and synthetic statements, and the reduction of theory to observation-statements. Quine presents himself as a pragmatist in the American tradition,[32] and says of physical objects that they are posits, inventions that we cannot do without, but epistemologically on the same level as the gods of Homer.[33] This is quite strong stuff, given the staunchly realist assumptions of most analytic philosophers at the time. So how are these views presented?

The style in these passages is strongly reminiscent of a chummy interview, in which the interviewee treats the interviewer as his friend. In an article, which this really is, the friendly treatment is for the reader.

> As an empiricist I continue to think of the conceptual scheme of science as a tool . . . Physical objects are conceptually imported into the situation as convenient intermediaries . . . simply as irreducible posits comparable, epistemologically, to the gods of Homer. For my part I do, qua lay physicist, believe in physical objects and not in Homer's gods. . . .[34]

The tone is almost chatty, and your defenses are weakened by hearing this from someone who sounds like a friend, and who introduces a funny remark with 'for my part . . .'. The reader is taken along by an avuncular figure who speaks directly to you. This stylistic feature follows us right to the end of the piece, where Quine still keeps the first-person address. 'I espouse a more thorough pragmatism', he says, and we are inclined to believe him.

'Two Dogmas . . .' is arguably one of the most influential contributions to twentieth-century philosophy, and the reasons for its success are not only the stringent arguments and the daring radical conclusions, but also the accessible and engaging style. But let us look at the relationship between content and style. One of the central features of Quine's alternative model is the web of belief, where only the edges of this web will have to be squared with experience. 'The rest, with all its elaborate myths and fictions, has as its objective the simplicity of laws'.[35] So where does Quine's contribution lie? We may say that it is not science anyway, and therefore it does not belong in this picture at all. However, Quine holds that philosophy and science are continuous, so it should. This contribution is not itself a part of the web of belief, but it is about the web of belief, and the relationships between experience and theory. For sure, it is not a series of observation sentences, which can be checked directly with experience. Perhaps it is more in line with the 'elaborate myths and fictions' of those parts of the web of belief which are not directly in contact with experience? If it is, how can it be at all different from literary works? After all, according to Quine himself, Homer's gods and scientific laws are very much on the same level in terms of epistemology, and if so: how can Quine's account of these relationships be more stringent or close to the verification-squad of experience than scientific laws? In short, should we put Homer and Quine on the same level, and treat their texts the same way?[36]

WHAT DOES IT ALL MEAN?

Our discussions of these three philosophers and their works have shown that the interactionist model Berel Lang has proposed, which he contrasted with a neutralist one, seems best equipped to deal fully with the range and variety of styles of philosophy. The dangers which he saw with this model, that by writing in diverse forms and styles philosophers cannot properly communicate with one another, cannot be quite true. Had it been, we would not have been able to conduct the discussions above. Plato and Wittgenstein are maybe extreme examples when it comes to style and form. Philosophy deals with arguments and clarification, but it is also a way of influencing minds. Written philosophy may do much to influence your mind without stating so in arguments that are easy to identify and evaluate. It is, however, possible to reconstruct arguments, and to identify the ways in which the text tries to shape its reception. In other words, to read the text as literature, and to analyse it using many of the same tools as we use in literary analysis.

This is not to say that the rhetoric of philosophy, the way the text is written, is easily translated into other forms. To argue that it does not matter what form or style the philosophical text takes, is to support the neutralist stance, that content is independent of and prior to both. The reader is influenced and perhaps persuaded by more than just convincing arguments. Examples may be the way Plato characterises Socrates and Phaedrus, and how the sophist Lysias is characterised through the content of the speech he has written. But also the sheer visual power of Quine's metaphor of the web of belief can assist in persuading the reader of the truth and relevance of the philosophical views of the author. The minimal perspective, the weak interactionist model, in discussing the rhetoric of philosophy is that we do well to remember that philosophy shares a box of tricks with literature and many other types of text, and that the style and form of works of philosophy influence readers independently of the clear and identifiable statements of the text. The wide-ranging perspective, or the strong interactionist model, is to maintain that form is irreducible and non reductive, that what is written as, say, a dialogue, cannot be understood and discussed in a different form, such as the scholarly article. That it seems possible here, in this book, to discuss the way Plato and Quine use their writings to influence the readers' perceptions of what they are proposing suggests that the strong interactionist model may be false. We are not confined to the form of the utterance, but can 'translate' into more mundane prose. But is this sort of translation of equal worth? For one thing it cannot persuade, enlighten and entertain in the same way. It is certainly a reduction, a reduction which leaves something behind. However, is not as radical as trying to paint a symphony or play a painting.

If it is the case that form contributes something irreducible to the content of philosophy, it is a loss that philosophy in the latter part of the twentieth century became rather limited in its range of genres and modes of expression. The uniformation of philosophy with regard to form would mean that this is a limitation of philosophy itself. But this situation is not all negative. Works of philosophy which are similar in style and form, like the 'normal' conference paper, or article in a journal, constitute a kind of lingua franca, a common formal and stylistic 'language' which makes it easier to communicate. When debating the same issues this may facilitate conjectures and refutations. Even if philosophy does not constitute a cumulative body of knowledge, mistakes, at least, can perhaps be more easily identified and corrected by colleagues.

The answer to the question in the chapter heading should be 'yes', qualified with 'we can and should read philosophical works with the same attention to formal and stylistic features as when we read literary works'. Does this mean that our approaches to philosophical texts and to literary ones should be the same? Can we expect the same of those two kinds of text, if they are different kinds of texts? To answer these questions we need to approach the issues from the other side as well, which is just what we are going to do in the next chapter.

FURTHER READING

Philosophy and Rhetoric is a journal published by Penn State Press, which has articles about the relationship between rhetoric and philosophy, and discussions of the philosophical aspects of argumentation.

Martin Warner's *Philosophical Finesse: Studies in the Art of Rational Persuasion* (Oxford: Clarendon Press, 1989) is a study of several cases from the history of philosophy, with particular attention to the kinds of persuasion which cannot be classified as either deductive or inductive. Pascal's notion of *finesse* is rehabilitated.

Berel Lang's books, *Philosophy and the Art of Writing: Studies in Philosophical and Literary Style* (Lewisburg: Bucknell University Press, 1983), *The Anatomy of Philosophical Style: Literary Philosophy and the Philosophy of Literature* (Oxford: Blackwell, 1990), are some of the most interesting studies on the style and form of philosophical writings.

On the 'literary' qualities of Plato's *Phaedrus*, G. R. F. Ferrari's *Listening to the Cicadas: A Study of Plato's 'Phaedrus'* (Cambridge: Cambridge University Press, 1987) remains a highly interesting study.

On the difference between philosophy and literature, discussed in the light of Derrida's challenges to such a distinction, I recommend Martin Warner's paper 'On Not Deconstructing the Difference Between Literature and Philosophy', *Philosophy and Literature*, 13 (1989), pp. 16–27.

NOTES

1. Literally, 'the wise' (*hoi sophoi*). Plato appears to have been ironic when he used this phrase about his opponents.
2. Bernard Williams, *Shame and Necessity* (Berkeley, CA: University of California Press, 1993), pp. 156–7. G. R. F. Ferrari claims that Plato accepts and acts on rhetoric's insistence that truth is impotent without persuasion, in *Listening to the Cicadas: A Study of Plato's 'Phaedrus'* (Cambridge: Cambridge University Press, 1987), p. 58.
3. Berel Lang, *The Anatomy of Philosophical Style: Literary Philosophy and the Philosophy of Literature* (Oxford: Blackwell, 1990).
4. Lang, *The Anatomy of Philosophical Style*, p. 12.
5. Jaques Derrida, 'Plato's Pharmacy', in *Dissemination*, trans. Barbara Johnson (London: Athlone Press, 1981), pp. 61–171. The book was first published in French in 1972.
6. In Ferrari's *Listening to the Cicadas*, pp. 214–22.

7. In this section I use some passages from my article 'The Critique of Writing in Plato's *Phaedrus*: A Meta-fictional Heuristic?', *Philosophical Writings*, 3 (1998), issue 8, pp. 3–13. I wish to thank the editors for their kind permission to use this material.

8. My references will be to Plato, *Phaedrus*, trans. R. Hackforth (Cambridge: Cambridge University Press, 1952).

9. Stanley Rosen, *Plato's Sophist: The Drama of Original and Image* (New Haven, CT: Yale University Press, 1983).

10. Rosen, p. 1.

11. There are several full-length studies of this dialogue, of which I find Ferrari's *Listening to the Cicadas* (see above) the most illuminating.

12. This may seem abhorrent today, and was beginning to seem less acceptable even at the time of Plato. There were, however, strict rules on how such relationships were to be conducted. One of the curious features was that sexual intercourse was only to take place between the thighs of the boy. If anal intercourse were to take place, the boy was considered to be a prostitute. Kenneth J. Dover's *Greek Homosexuality* (London: Duckworth, 1978) is the authoritative work on these relationships.

13. G. R. F. Ferrari, 'Plato and Poetry', in George A. Kennedy (ed.), *The Cambridge History of Literary Criticism, Vol. 1: Classical Criticism* (Cambridge: Cambridge University Press, 1989), pp. 145–6.

14. A more elaborate version of this reading of the *Phaedrus* can be found in my own 'The Critique of Writing in Plato's *Phaedrus*: A Meta-fictional Heuristic?' (see above).

15. Ludwig Wittgenstein, *Tractatus Logico-Philosophicus*, trans. D. F. Pears and B. F. McGuinness (London: Routledge, 1961), first published in German in *Annalen der Naturphilosophie*, 1921. References are to paragraphs, given in the main text.

16. Wittgenstein, *Tractatus*, p. 5.

17. 1.1 is a comment on 1, and 1.11 and 1.12 are both comments on 1.1, while 1.2 is a comment on 1, but not on 1.13; 2 is a new statement.

18. Ludwig Wittgenstein, *Philosophical Investigations*, trans. G. E. M. Anscombe (Oxford: Blackwell, 1953). References to this work are generally to numbered paragraphs and not to pages.

19. Wittgenstein's preface (written in 1945) to the *Investigations*, p. vii.

20. Wittgenstein, *Investigations*, 109.

21. Ludwig Wittgenstein, *Culture and Value*, G. H. von Wright (ed.), trans. Peter Winch, revised edn by Alois Pichler (Oxford: Blackwell, 1998), p. 77e.

22. Willard van Orman Quine, *The Time of My Life* (Cambridge, MA: MIT Press, 1985).

23. Willard van Orman Quine, *From a Logical Point of View* (Cambridge, MA: Harvard University Press, 1953), pp. 20–46.

24. Quine, 'Two Dogmas . . .', p. 20.

25. Quine, 'Two Dogmas . . .', p. 21.

26. Quine was later to use the notion of 'web', as in the title of the short book he co-authored with J. S. Ullian, *The Web of Belief* (New York: Random House, 1970). Quine came to see this as a good metaphor for what he expressed as early as in 'Two Dogmas of Empiricism', and I shall also use this term in the following discussion.

27. Quine, 'Two Dogmas . . .', p. 41. This has also been argued by the French philosopher Pierre Duhem, as Quine himself points out.

28. Quine, 'Two Dogmas . . .', p. 43.

29. Jaques Derrida, 'White Mythology', in *Margins of Philosophy*, trans. Alan Bass (Brighton: Harvester Press, 1982), pp. 207–71. First published in French in 1972.

30. Derrida, 'White Mythology', p. 271.

31. For a discussion of Derrida's views in 'White Mythology', see Martin Warner's 'On Not Deconstructing the Difference Between Literature and Philosophy', *Philosophy and Literature*, 13 (1989), pp. 16–27.

32. This tradition goes back to Charles Sanders Peirce and William James (the brother of Henry James). To simplify, this direction in philosophy held, among other views, that any distinction made in language was meaningless unless it also made a difference in observable practice.

33. Quine, 'Two Dogmas . . .', p. 44.

34. Quine, 'Two Dogmas . . .', p. 44.

35. Quine, 'Two Dogmas . . .', p. 45.

36. Always ignoring the fact that Homer never wrote a word.

SEVEN

PHILOSOPHY IN LITERATURE?

We have seen that what are often considered to be 'literary' ways of reading can also illuminate philosophical texts of different epochs and orientations. Now we shall look more closely at possible ways in which literary works may be seen to further the understanding of problems and questions usually considered to be philosophical.

There may be many ways in which literary works can contribute to philosophy. Jostein Gaarder's *Sophie's World: A Novel about the History of Philosophy*[1] became a best-seller world-wide with the story of a girl who, to simplify a little, takes a correspondence course in philosophy. This is, as the sub-title indicates, a novel with philosophy thrown in. Alternatively it is philosophy with some fictional framing – depending on how you see it. This is a problem only if you desperately need to have all books neatly fitted into mutually exclusive slots. The main questions in this chapter revolve around whether and how some mainstream literary works can contribute to, and maybe constitute, philosophical inquiry. Both of our main examples of how literature is conceived to contribute to philosophy, or to the common concerns of both philosophy and literature, are American philosophers. First Martha Craven Nussbaum who argues that some literary works are indispensable to moral philosophy, and then Stanley Cavell whose work in philosophy and literature has been highly influential.

MARTHA NUSSBAUM, NOVELS AND ETHICS

Certain truths about human life can only be fittingly and accurately stated in the language and forms characteristic of the narrative artist.[2]

This is the core of Martha Craven Nussbaum's claim that some literary works are indispensable to philosophy, or more precisely moral philosophy. Her ideas about philosophy and literature have been put forward in several books and articles, but here we shall concentrate on the collection *Love's Knowledge: Essays on Philosophy and Literature*. Her view is that in literary narrative life is represented *as* something – in a style which sets up *certain reactions in the reader* which are suitable for understanding these truths about life. This is behind the recent renewal of interest in the relationships between literature and philosophy. Partly responsible for this recourse to literature is a perceived dryness in academic philosophy. This may not matter much if the topic is logic or even some other sub-divisions of philosophy such as metaphysics, but when the topic of discussion is how we should behave and react to one another as human beings, which is the topic of moral philosophy, the arid prose of academic philosophy is not up to the task, according to Nussbaum.

It is significant that Nussbaum is a classical scholar, and the classics is a field where literature and philosophy more naturally interact than in philosophy as it developed in the twentieth century. Her background, from her school-days, steeped her in the literary classics, and Nussbaum claims that she was doing moral philosophy without philosophy in school – through discussing the trials and tribulations of characters in literary texts.[3] So it would seem that for her literature and philosophy can be one and the same, in that in the field of moral philosophy they are dealing with the same issues. Still, they are not doing this in the same way, or there would be little sense in saying that philosophical questions were pursued in a different form. Nussbaum's claim is, rather, that some literary works have a specific – a literarily specific – place in moral philosophy as such. The claim is quite strong: that this position is unique in ethics – no other discourse is appropriate, and it implies that ethics is incomplete without literature. So, literature can instruct, though the way literature does this is different from other kinds of writing. Nussbaum does not suggest that literature and philosophy are indistinct, on the contrary: it is the distinct form of some literary works which make them crucially important to the pursuit of philosophical questions, questions which cannot be pursued through the traditional forms of philosophy.

As far as form is concerned, it is indeed interesting to see how her own writing is indicative of the direction her more identifiable positions suggest. She stays autobiographical, assuming that what she read during a certain phase of her life is of interest to us, and to what she is saying about philosophy and literature. To some this may seem self-obsessed, but it is in keeping with her views on form and content. It is the meeting of the individual with the literary works – which she calls her friends – that is of prime importance. One may wonder why real-life persons cannot have the same role, why only the pseudo lives of fictional characters can perform this role in moral philosophy. After all, in the case of real people, the level of specificity should be greater, and the call for empathy even stronger. No literary character has actually suffered, so why cannot an autobiography or a biography of someone who has actually lived perform the same role?

The answer for Nussbaum is the authorial presence. Some thought the author was dead, as we saw in Chapter 4, but Nussbaum certainly gives this figure the kiss of life. According to her, the authorial voice occupies in thought and feeling the reader's position – asking what the reader should/could think and feel. This does not involve the authors' life and biography, but only the authorial presence as they animate the text.[4] Nussbaum claims to be only concerned with what is embodied in the text, and that critical statements made by the author have no authority beyond statements of other critics.[5] However, given that authors have full discretion in what is embodied in the text, this seems to give them a fair degree of authority over the reader, something which comes through when she writes of the artist that 'when we follow him as attentive readers, we ourselves engage in ethical conduct, and our readings themselves are assessable ethical acts'.[6]

Nussbaum claims to be interested in all and only those thoughts, feelings, wishes, movements and other processes that are actually there in the text.[7] However, in the text you only see words and sentences, and all the other properties you attribute to the text you have to infer from your understanding of what those words mean in the context. This means that what you have to attend to are not only those words and sentences present to your eyes as they follow the text, but also those your memory will furnish you with, and this requires an understanding of what has gone before, which in turns requires a preconception of the whole of the work. In other words, the hermeneutics of reading, which we discussed in Chapter 5, suggests that 'what is actually there' in the text is in great measure also a product of the reader's ability to make sense of what is being read, a process which is not only dependent on the words the author has put in the text, but also on the reader's own personality and concerns. This is a more dynamic interaction between reader and writer than Nussbaum seems to allow for. In her conception it seems that one end of the literary process has all the power, and it is this lack of a proper space for the reader which is one of the most problematic aspects of her theories. She even goes so far as to say that 'in the reading of a literary text, there is a standard of correctness set by the author's sense of life, as it finds its way into the work'.[8]

Why this emphasis on the author? I think the answer may be found in the same direction as that to the question of why she does not allow much space for the activity of the reader: it is the voice of the authorial presence and the 'spin' he or she may give that is at issue. It's the author's conception that is of the essence with regard to the moral import of literature. Reasons for holding such a view may be found in Nussbaum's conception of ethics, which is an Aristotelian one. For Aristotle, ethics was the question of how to live your life, as we saw in the presentation of his ethics in Chapter 2. His ethics has a practical element, there are no formulae, no precepts, which can tell you how to live your life, and his emphasis is very practical. In a way you 'become what you do', in that you form habits through your actions. It is rare that you have the time to deliberate for a long time when you are confronted with a choice, so settled habits are important. However, the situations we are confronted with are various, and you are never likely to enter into a situation which in all its particulars is identical to any situation you were in before. For Nussbaum it may be that it is Aristotle's emphasis on the particulars of a situation which is the key to the importance of literature for moral philosophy. What it is right to do depends not only on what it is generally right to do, what the ethical norms are, but also on what the specific circumstances of any situation are. It is this ability to see what is demanded of you generally in the light of the specific situation you are in, and vice versa, which it is particularly important to cultivate. You do not only learn from living your own life, and learning the norms of your culture, you also learn through others, in particular through the example of your elders.

This learning how to live through others is particularly evident in Nussbaum's writings when she emphasises that (at least some) literary works are, almost literally, *her friends*, which is evident in her essays concerning the various literary works she loves (chiefly those by Henry James and Charles Dickens). However, if you are going to learn from your friends, it is important to pick the right ones. The elders of ancient Greek culture were thought to possess wisdom through their age and experience; they were more or less defined as ethical experts. There are both good and bad friends, however, and in picking your friends you also pick important influences on the development of your personality. As Richard A. Posner, an American judge with an interest in literature, says: 'literature offers a vast choice of friendships. Many of them are with evil, dangerous, or irresponsible people – *awful* role models'.[9] His criticism of Nussbaum's position is that she gives literature a seriously one-sided image, where only its solemn and puritanical side is allowed to show. Literature is much more varied than the selection Nussbaum uses as her focus, so the question is whether immersion in literature *as such* make us better people, or if it is a question of picking out the right friends. It is likely that for Nussbaum it is the latter. 'No claim about novels in general, far less about literature in general, could possibly emerge from this book', she writes. Still, it is a beginning, she claims, and one rooted in '*my* love for *certain* novels and in *my* closely related concern with *certain* problems'.[10] The latter quotation makes this discussion suddenly restricted to a narrow range of personal interests, but she invites, nevertheless, the wider questions of the moral or ethical worth of literature as such, and in particular the genre of the novel. Later in the introduction her restrictions seem to be forgotten when she stresses that novels are particularly apt to take up the necessary role of an adjunct to moral philosophy (p. 46). They have the emotive appeal, absorbing plottedness, and the ability to make of you a friend. But these qualities, it should be remembered, tend to reduce the imaginative distance between yourself and what is being considered – they erode the critical faculties, and were some of the most important reasons why Plato wanted to banish the poets and the rhapsodes from his ideal republic, as seen in Chapter 2. Yet, these are the reasons why Nussbaum wants to have them reinstated, not only in the republic of today, but also as a part of ethical deliberation. But not just any novel, poem or play. Nussbaum stresses that 'these larger questions can best be approached through the detailed study of complex particular cases',[11] i.e. that what she has to say should be judged against the background of her particular engagement with particular works. It is difficult, perhaps impossible, to take up the challenge without going into the particularities of her concrete engagement with certain works, which we are going to do a little later.

But if literary works can be your friends, and Posner is right about the variable quality and dependability of literary friends, how do we succeed in finding the good friends except through hanging out with a bad lot from time to time? After all, you cannot know these friends before getting to know them, and in getting to know them they may start to influence you. In judging which friends are the good ones, you have to use your own moral judgements, which then have to be prior to the acquaintance. This leads to circularity, which can be both virtuous and vicious, depending either on the quality of your judgements, or on pure luck. The alternative Nussbaum seems to prefer is to take the quality of the literary friendships on trust. The tradition, or possibly the moral experts, know which friendships are good for you, but this only takes the previous dilemma of who to trust one step further.

One solution would be to trust Nussbaum, of course, and enter into friendships with the works of James and Dickens, but as we shall see shortly this solution also comes with problems of its own. The classics would, through their status, seem to be the choice of the tradition, but most classics do not seem to have much of an edge when it comes to be awarded the status as edifying works:

> Do we stalk out of *Hamlet* at the end of the first scene, when we discover there is a *ghost* in an ostensibly adult play? Why then should we stalk out of *Othello* when we discover that it depicts a racially mixed marriage as possibly unnatural? . . . Most readers accept the presence of obsolete ethics in literature with the same equanimity that they accept the presence of obsolete military technology or antiquated diction or customs in literature, as things both inevitable, given the antiquity of so much literature, and incidental to the purpose for which we read literature.[12]

The classics seem to be classics for reasons other than their clear support for the moral values of the early twenty-first century. The canon of the established great works of western literature has, of course, been questioned for this reason.[13] The values inherent in this canon are seen to be out of touch with the values of modern society, and the critics of the canon claim that by forcing these works on the young people of today the schools and universities perpetuate misogynist and anti-egalitarian values still dominant even in present-day western societies. So the classics, considered as a collective body of works, cannot be considered trustworthy as moral guides, and Nussbaum makes sure that she does not suggest this. After all, literature is a moral anarchy, with frequent bouts of patricide, murder, human sacrifice, adultery, deceit, racism, anti-Semitism, not to mention torture, rape and suicide. The works she considers are only her own choices, chosen, one would assume, on the basis of her own moral standards. But these moral standards are also present in her reading of the chosen works. We have seen in Chapter 5 that the process of literary interpretation is complex, and that different epochs, cultures and people come up with different interpretations of the same work. The choices and emphases in literary interpretation are also important in what the reader takes the work to 'teach' in terms of moral significance. Far from teaching one moral lesson, even the works Nussbaum selects as suitable moral guides can be read in different and even conflicting ways. Henry James is one of the authors she chooses, because of his distinctive ethical view, which is one she also associates with Aristotle. This ethical view involves the cognitive role of the emotions (that you must learn to feel the feelings appropriate to a situation in order to act correctly in it), and an insistence on the importance of the contextual complexity of these situations. Her claim is that in order to investigate this Aristotelian view fully, we should turn to texts where this view is adequately explored, and these texts are by their very nature literary ones and not those of arid academic prose.[14] So let us have a look, then, at her reading of one of Henry James's novels, *The Golden Bowl*. The following presentation is inspired both by Nussbaum's reading and analysis in *Love's Knowledge* and Richard Posner's criticism of the same.[15]

In this novel, Maggie, a very rich young American woman, marries a penniless Italian prince who, unknown to her, is in love with Charlotte, an American woman who is both poor and Maggie's best friend. Charlotte marries Maggie's father, while continuing her relationship with the prince. Maggie discovers that her husband is committing adultery with Charlotte, and manages to reclaim her husband and send Charlotte packing. It is also important that Maggie's bond to her wealthy father is perhaps stronger than is healthy for her or anybody else. This complicated situation is partly seen through the eyes of the 'square' Assinghams.

Nussbaum argues that *The Golden Bowl* is a novel

> about the development of a woman. To be a woman, to give herself to her husband, Maggie will need to come to see herself as something cracked, imperfect, unsafe, a vessel with a hole through which water may pass, a steamer compartment no longer tightly sealed.[16]

This 'aboutness' is quite revealing. What one sees the novel to be about is quite crucial to the question of what kind of moral lessons to draw, and to what kind of guidance it can provide in the pursuit of that all important question of how to live your life. Literary works which support only one possible interpretation do so at the peril of appearing rather flat and boring. It is therefore possible to have rather different interpretations of the novel. This must pose a problem for Nussbaum and others who claim that literature can teach moral lessons. It is, for instance, possible to see a variety of moral perspectives in *The Golden Bowl*, and not all of them wholesome. One may, for instance, side with the adulterers. After all, they experience true love, and from this perspective Maggie is an insufferably stuffy rich girl who wins out in the end due to her inherited wealth. The prince can be seen as a gold-digger, and Maggie can quite legitimately be seen as weak, both for marrying the prince in the first place, and for accepting his adultery. Maggie's close relationship with her father can quite legitimately be seen as close to incestuous, and modern sentiments may well find their condescension to the impecunious Prince and

Charlotte unbearable. These different 'takes' can coexist quite happily. The novel is rich, and to focus, like Nussbaum, only on a fine selection of the moral aspects may be to miss the Gothic vein in James's imagination – the lurid, the unnatural and the quasi-incestuous. There is voyeurism, there is the daughter condoning her husband's adultery with her stepmother, who is a good friend, and father and daughter aware of and managing the adultery. Perhaps aware of this, Nussbaum does, however, argue that sometimes a very brief fiction is sufficient for the morally relevant sort of inquiry, though sometimes the length and complexity of a novel is necessary,[17] but she does not argue that there is something irreducibly literary which has to be present in order for these extensive accounts, fictional or otherwise, to do the ethically salient work. This is relevant in the discussion over how essential the literariness of literature is for its role in ethics, and whether or not other genres could serve us just as well.

The aestheticians Peter Lamarque and Stein Haugom Olsen distinguish between philosophy *in* literature and philosophy *through* literature, and argue that there is a particular literary stance or approach, which is not compatible with other approaches, such as an interest in the historical context of the work or the personality of the author.[18] They claim that if you read for moral illumination you do not read it *as* a literary work, but more as an imaginative and emotive working out of morally/ethically charged situations, where the literariness of literature is of no relevance. The literary work may be an eye opener, a reminder or an example, but that is not 'philosophy in literature', but 'philosophy through literature' according to Lamarque and Olsen, because its literariness, the properties specific to literature, are not necessary to it.[19] Still, one of Nussbaum's central claims is that form contains a view of human life, and it is the form of literature which makes it important in the kind of ethical quest of self-discovery she advocates. She is worried that at present there is not even a quarrel between philosophy and literature, since the two seem to exist in splendid isolation. Here the question of form is highly important. The dry prose of academic philosophy stands in the way of any real appreciation of the closeness of the two, and on the literary side of the academy the situation has in the recent past not been any more hospitable. New critics focused on form and close reading, and explicitly discouraged any attempt at developing a relationship between literature and life, while structuralists and deconstructionists have been no less arid and academic than the philosophers. Indeed, some of their practitioners have attempted to take on the mantle of philosophy, while arguing that not only literature, but also language as such, could not have any connection with anything outside itself.[20] Given this picture, it is no wonder that Nussbaum has made her mark. Many students of literature have started out interested in literature because they have felt that at least some works really changed the way they saw things, and that some kind of insight was arrived at that you could not get by any other means. This is what Nussbaum seems to argue, and many of us would like her to be right.

But we have to remember that Nussbaum is careful in her pronouncements, and that she does not advance any theses about literature as such, but only about the quality and usefulness of some selected works. Still, are there any reasons to think that literature is a more certain path than any other to knowledge and wisdom about humanity and society, and indeed, 'how to live one's life'? No doubt, there are people who would rather learn about this from novels than from, say, other people, biographies, history – even science – but it does not follow from this that novels are better. Then there are those who take exception to literature being used as moral guidance, such as the critic Helen Vendler: 'treating fictions as moral peppills or moral emetics is repugnant to anyone who realizes the complex psychological and moral motives of a work of art'.[21] However, literature may enlarge our empathetic awareness of ethical questions, and the situations where crucial choices have to be made, though of course that does not in itself make the reader a better person. It is quite possible that one may get to understand people and moral choices better, only to take advantage and further the cause of evil and depravity in the world. Knowing what is right is no guarantee for doing it. It may only foster new ways of avoiding getting caught. Just consider the popularity of courses in business ethics: one may suspect that they function more as massage for the ethical conscience of executives than as templates for good practice. It is often not lack of knowledge of what is morally right that is at stake in business – it is the will to do it.

Even if Nussbaum's version of the importance of literature for our moral being is problematic, there are other alternatives. Consider Peter Brooks who says that:

> our lives are ceaselessly intertwined with narratives, with the stories that we tell and hear told, those we dream or imagine or would like to tell, all of which are reworked in that story of our own lives that we narrate to ourselves in an episodic, sometimes semiconscious, but virtually uninterrupted monologue.[22]

There are several philosophers who have focused on the possible narrative structure of our conceptions of ourselves, such as Paul Ricoeur, Alasdair

MacIntyre and Charles Taylor, and Richard Eldridge.[23] In his book *On Moral Personhood: Philosophy, Literature, Criticism and Self-Understanding*[24] Eldridge wants to develop a narrativist conception of persons and agency: 'If it is plausible to see an internal relation between personhood and literary narrative, then it is further plausible to see something of a common personhood variously manifested in different narratives'.[25] Eldridge is more of a Kantian than Nussbaum, he is less concerned with particular persons and their particular choices than she is, and looks for more general answers to the eternal questions such as 'how to live ones life'. It is this kind of engagement which is manifested in the readings in his book, of Conrad, Wordsworth, Coleridge and Jane Austin. In each of these texts, 'the route toward partial resolution and self-understanding is presented as involving multiple and ongoing activities of reading and interpreting'.[26]

Eldridge sees the characters in literature as testing-ground for the acceptability of ethical theories, since given the commonality of the narrative structure these characters are examples of lived lives. Thus, it is open to question whether or not Nussbaum and Eldridge are agreed on the role of literature in moral philosophy. While Nussbaum wants to argue for 'literature as moral philosophy', as an integrated part of moral philosophy, it seems fair to see Eldridge as representing the view of 'moral philosophy through literature'. He claims that any narrative is of moral interest and worth, given that the constitution of personhood is structured narratively.[27] However, this means that it is not the specifically *literary* element that is of importance – it is the narrative, the lived life, and the development through experience and reflection.

Eldridge's position comes very close to saying that we can learn from example, which does not take us much further in our quest to find philosophy in literature. There may be another possibility, though. Perhaps reading literature, particularly novels, exercises our perceptions and our abilities to judge people and situations so as to act adequately. Perhaps these skills are *both* literary skills, i.e. skills necessary to get the kind of enjoyment from a literary work that makes it a particular kind of production, *and* moral skills – skills that are necessary to live as empathetic and responsible social beings. The ability to see, to pick out the relevant elements of any situation, is quite crucial to Nussbaum. In her reading of Aristotle she emphasises the priority of the particular, and one of her favourite quotation from Aristotle is that 'the discrimination lies in perception'.[28] It is this ability to perceive the particular in a situation that is a precondition for choosing a course of action, and the right kind of attention to the right kind of literature may be beneficial in this respect, but so may other kinds of writing.

Against this it may be claimed that reading does not cause you to act – in fact you do not respond in a literary manner if you do react and do something with what is happening. This, however, is what you should do as a responsible social being. There also seems to be a lack of forceful empirical examples of literature improving your extra-literary abilities as a social and moral being. It is well known that people well versed in the classics were among those who were responsible for exterminating millions of people during the Second World War. If their reading of literature enlarged their empathetic abilities, or their abilities to discern the morally relevant features of the situations, it did not appear to affect their actions. It could be argued, though, that these people could not have attended properly to the literary works they had read. However, less seriously, people who spend most of their time reading, interpreting and teaching literary works, the staff of literature departments around the world, are not known to be either better or worse people than others. In fact, one of our number, K. K. Ruthven, is prepared to say that 'despite their familiarity with the classics, professors of literature do not appear to lead better lives than other people, and frequently display unbecoming virulence on the subject of one another's shortcomings'.[29] It is possible, though, that Nussbaum is right when she claims that this is because professors are jaded and detached, and do not read with the immersion characteristic of ordinary readers,[30] but it is also possible that John Horton is right when he says that we have to remember that literature is *just* stories, and that 'literature may allow us to experience our emotions "on the cheap", and ultimately encourage a peculiarly aesthetic deformation of our moral sensibilities'.[31]

At this point we had better remind ourselves of what we have been discussing here. Nussbaum's main point is that some novels, read and commented on in a certain way, should be seen as integrated elements of moral philosophy. This is because they offer the kind of friendship that may guide our moral development, fulfilling much the same function as 'elders' in Aristotelian thinking. They present characters in their full significance, complete with emotional engagement, in a particularity that can only be rivalled by life itself. Emotion is cognitive, according to the Aristotelianism of Nussbaum, with its emphasis on learning habits and the particularised circumstances of moral choices, and you learn to feel the appropriate emotions in given circumstances. This is a necessary part of moral philosophy, since moral philosophy in its academic version often is dry, abstract and removed from lived experience. Form is itself a statement,[32] and certain truths about the world can only be uttered in the forms of the narrative artists.[33] Literature allows us to live vicariously – in an intensified atmosphere that calls on our rational and emotional participation, and which may further our moral understanding to such a degree that it is a necessary part of moral philosophy.

On the other hand, Nussbaum relies on a naive account of reading and interpretation, and relies maybe too much on the presence of the author-genius. This may obscure the creative role of the reader in the reading process, and the quite considerable likelihood that the 'ethical position is in place before the literary reading begins, and furnishes the criteria of choice and shapes interpretation'.[34] In arguing the role of literature in expanding our emotional and cognitive capacities, Nussbaum also trusts the quality of empathy, but empathy may be, and often is, amoral. Vicarious experience may enrich, but it does not, as such, ennoble. Literature does indeed have the capacity to expand our horizons, and to make us understand motivations and world-pictures different from our own. Perhaps this is likely to be the most salutary effect of literature, rather than its supposed ennobling effect. From cogitation to action there is a leap no amount of reading high-calibre literature may be able to bridge. We seem to want both profound insights and an enjoyable read, and for most people reading good literature is more pleasurable than reading even good moral philosophy. Perhaps the views of Nussbaum and others about the value of reading good literature were so welcome that we wanted them to be true? For those of us who have spent a lot of time reading and enjoying literary works it would indeed be welcome to hear that this activity has made us better people. This in itself should make us aware of a tendency, perhaps, to accept these views a little too readily.

Some may even feel that there is something 'olde world' and author-itarian about the view that people should read some chosen literary works of the Victorian era to make them better people. Could it be that Franz Kafka is closer to modern sentiments when he states in a letter that:

> I think we ought to read only the kind of books that wound and stab us . . . We need the books that affect us like a disaster, that grieve us deeply, like the death of someone we loved more than ourselves, like being banished into forests far from everyone, like a suicide. A book must be the axe for the frozen sea inside us. That is my belief.[35]

Were we to follow Kafka's recommendations, we would have a relation-ship between literature and philosophy different from the one we get through Nussbaum. Kafka seems to think that literature works, or should work, as a kind of provocation, not as a friend who gently guides us to see social situations in a particularly refined way. In this Kafka's view shows similarities with those of the philosopher Bernard Harrison, who argues that the 'mission' of literature is not to 'impart Great Truths but to unhinge and destabilize them'.[36] Kafka's view seems to be that we should remain open to literature, while Nussbaum wants to harness a limited set of texts into the use of moral philosophy. Not that these two approaches need to be mutually exclusive, but they are very different in that they seem to imply two distinct conceptions of personhood. One slightly patronising, the voice of authors guiding us through their moral vision. The other radical, maybe even anarchic, relying on the force of literature to provoke thoughts and questions, even powerful emotions, that can effect changes in the reader – changes that will differ from reader to reader, and which will be impossible to foresee. Questions of a philosophical nature are provoked, but no way or approach is necessarily suggested by the work. This latter perspective opens us up to the full negative force that a literary narrative can muster, while Nussbaum's perspective is circumscribed, looking for the education of sensibility and moral awareness. Neither of these perspectives can be seen as superior, or even the only perspectives there can be on 'philosophy in literature', as should be clear from our discussions in Chapter 5 about the nature of literary interpretation.

Were we to follow Kafka's recommendation and read only the books that 'affect us like a disaster', our literary diet would be at least as limited as that suggested by Nussbaum. It would, however, probably include Shakespeare's *King Lear*, which the philosopher Stanley Cavell analyses in a way that destabilises deep elements in our culture. Cavell's perspective on 'philosophy in literature' is both more fruitful and more demanding than those discussed above.

STANLEY CAVELL

Stanley Cavell even wants to destabilise the relationship between philosophy and literature, and to put philosophy and literature on an even footing. This he does not do through abstruse pronouncements, but by interpreting some of Shakespeare's plays, notably *King Lear*.

Cavell is an American philosopher and cultural theorist born in 1926 in Atlanta, Georgia. His philosophically active life has been spent first in New York and then in Boston, where he is Professor at Harvard University. He started out with an interest in the implications of ordinary language philosophy, associated with Wittgenstein and the Oxford philosopher John L. Austin. This interest was the basis for his work in aesthetics, in particular, and also in film-studies.[37] His interest in the criteria of use of ordinary language is coupled with that of the various manifestations in modern culture of the sceptical impulse. Cavell claims that this sceptical impulse is not only to be found in philosophy, where its manifestations originated in classical philosophy (Sextus Empiricus), and reached its zenith in Descartes and Hume, but also in literature. Its pervasiveness in the Shakespearean corpus has been pointed out by Cavell, and been greeted with great interest not least from literary scholars. This latter involvement will be the main focus of the present exposition and discussion. It should be clear from the outset, however, that Cavell is more of what we might call a 'suggestive philosopher', and not one for clear and authoritarian pronouncements. At the risk of misrepresenting his views, I shall try to make what he has to say more explicit than in his own writings, and the focus will be the collection of articles *Disowning Knowledge*, chiefly the famous essay 'The Avoidance of Love: A Reading of *King Lear*'.[38]

To begin with, we have to get some kind of idea of what kind of scepticism Cavell is focusing on. There are many forms of scepticism, among which the extremes can be labelled partial and global. The global scepticism is the most extreme, and it implies that we cannot be sure that we know anything. Not certainly, not even likely. Partial, or regional, skepticism holds only that there are kinds of knowledge that are impossible to have or prove, be it in certain areas (such as knowledge of our own or of other minds), or certain degrees. Cavell's diverse contributions can be said to unite in the view that scepticism in its various guises is a self-inflicted threat to human existence which derives from existential concerns. Cavell thinks scepticism is the most recent and the most destructive version of the ancient wish to escape the human being's situation within language and history. Philosophical skepticism is only the most refined form of a type of scepticism which is prevalent in many spheres throughout history.

In the French rationalist philosopher Descartes' writings, scepticism is manifested mainly as self-doubt. The result of his search for the indubitable bedrock on which knowledge can be founded is common knowledge: *cogito, ergo sum* (I think, therefore I am). In Shakespeare's works, according to Cavell, the sceptical doubt is mainly manifested as a doubt regarding other minds and the intelligibility of not only the Universe, but even the local, social universe (such as in *Hamlet*). More than anything, this is doubted in the observance, and it is no accident that this book is called 'disowning knowledge'. Cavell is convinced, not only that scepticism is a topic within the Shakespearean corpus, but that this mode of drama in itself constitutes an effort to overcome the sceptical impulse in our culture. The simplest way to state the relationship is that form and content mirror each other. The more elaborate formulation is that there is a doubling of the issues within the plays, and in the issues generated in and by an audience's relation to the plays themselves.

The kind of scepticism we see at work in *King Lear* is explained in Cavell's interpretation of what goes on in the first scene of the first act, where Lear calls for declarations of love from his daughters. Cavell claims that the events in *King Lear* are driven by Lear's inability to acknowledge the love of his youngest daughter. He is unable or unwilling to respond to that love, and unable or unwilling to reveal or otherwise face this fact about himself. He must therefore also go on avoiding recognising or acknowledging others, and deny the reality of their relation to him. In a way, he deprived them of this aspect of their reality when he forced the daughters to publicly declare their love for him in order to get a cut of the land. The two elder sisters, Goneril and Regan, declare their love in extravagant terms, while continuing to hate him. Cordelia finds herself unable to play up to the hypocrisy of her sisters, and replies 'nothing, my Lord' to her father's request for declarations of love. Lear fails to acknowledge that this is all she can say in a context where the words of love have taken on the opposite meaning through the false pronouncements of her sisters. He cannot acknowledge Cordelia's 'nothing, my Lord' as an expression of a wish not to compromise what they have together, since that would mean he would acknowledge that he could never pay for her love through material bribes, or make sure that he deserved it or know that he would keep it. Her pronouncement, had he acknowledged it for what it is, would mean a lack of certainty he cannot face. The result is that Cordelia is disinherited and banished from the country, and the events of the rest of the play follow with seeming necessity. However, this does not answer why scepticism is at work in the play, and least of all does it address why it is that Cavell thinks this play actually interprets scepticism, in that it yields to interpretation in terms of scepticism.[39]

'We need to forego knowledge', seems to be a central *motif* in *King Lear*. In the introduction to *The Claim of Reason*, perhaps Cavell's key work, he suggests that there is a 'reciprocation between the ideas of acknowledgement and of avoidance, for example as the thought that skepticism concerning other minds is not skepticism but is tragedy'.[40] In order to understand this, we must examine what happens when we watch a play. Our position is structurally analogous to that of the characters of the play: 'the medium is one which keeps all significance continuously before our eyes, so that when it comes over us that we have missed it, this discovery will reveal our ignorance to have been wilful, complicitous, a refusal to see'.[41] However, we know that these characters are not real –

they are fictional. They do not have the histories they claim to have. The person on the stage as King Lear is not really a king, but an actor. But what, then, is the particular nature of the existence of fictional characters? Well, for a start, we are not in the presence of the characters, but they are in ours. We should acknowledge characters in a play. Acknowledgement in the theatre does not amount to treating them as real people, as we would were we to intervene when that ghastly Othello is about to smother Desdemona. Inside the convention of theatre one does not, for example, have to reveal oneself to another in response to his or her pain. That is required outside, and constitutes the difference between reacting to the pain and acknowledging it. So how can acknowledgement be made complete in the theatre? One way is to respond as if to the time of the play – any prior knowledge of the ending cannot influence the reaction to any single event in the play prior to the ending. The same applies if you apply moral principles that do not take into account the particular responses of a character. Those are examples of a failure to acknowledge the characters as particular individuals, as people.

What is the parallel to self-revelation in the theatre, then? Acknowledgement of another involves this, but how can that be effected in the fictional and highly conventional setting of the theatre? What you reveal, according to Cavell, is that you are stationary, fixed and helpless to relieve their suffering. Only if you have understood the cause of their suffering do you acknowledge it, if not, you're just withholding your help and assistance. Cavell is suggesting a similarity between the cognitive element of acknowledgement in the theatre, and the necessarily active character of acknowledgement in real life. Your total separateness is what makes the characters on stage present, according to this model. Cavell thinks that this situation can make us better prepared to reveal our full humanity in situations outside the theatre, that this respite allows us to hold back, to stop, and perhaps engage our cognitive faculties.

Cavell sees the reading of Shakespeare, and particularly attending a play, as a form of redemptive activity. We live out a sceptical relation to the characters in the theatre. At the same time, it literalises the conditions we create by succumbing to scepticism outside the theatre, and so makes the nature of the rest of our existence plain, but by making our failure to reveal ourselves *de rigueur* in that setting, it also makes our overcoming of scepticism more feasible, and it may be that this overcoming can be extended beyond the walls of the theatre. According to Cavell this is a mode of poetic drama that Shakespeare offers his society as a medium of recovery from scepticism. It creates a place within which people can affirm the fact of the breach of unity in their situation.

If this is the case, why was not this thematic of the disowning of knowledge not seen by others prior to Cavell? This is actually a question he poses himself,[42] and is the sort of question one can pose about any perceptive reading. One answer could be that it is so obvious. The need to seek the far-fetched is perhaps the strongest imperative of literary criticism. However, we may also raise the question of whether Cavell himself, in his reading of *King Lear*, may be seen to manifest the kind of craving for absolute knowledge that is at the root of the sceptical impulse in life. In Cavell's blend of literary criticism and philosophy this may be seen in his need to make explicit every nuance and feature of the text: to clarify what is murky, and to draw to our attention the ignored elements of the text, and particularly the phenomenology of performance and audience reactions. At our level of meta-investigation, it may seem that Cavell, like Descartes before him, forgot to question his own venture in the same light. As Descartes forgot to question whether the evil spirit changed the sense of his words from one moment to the next, is it possible that Cavell has missed the craving for absolute knowledge of the literary text that may bring with it a tragic fall, as the literary text fails to yield what was asked of it?

We have arrived at the point where we should address the question of how literature and philosophy interact in Cavell's work on Shakespeare. In the introduction to his book, Cavell writes that he wishes to unsettle the matter of priority between philosophy and literature.[43] Cavell, through his reading of Shakespeare, interprets and deepens our understanding of the sceptical problematic in a way that it is hard to see that 'standard' academic philosophy in its various versions could do. Does this mean that literature can provide philosophy with work to do, or provide a kind of refinement, though not clarification, of the problems of the field? If so, it has not so far resulted in a new area within philosophy. There is no discussion of Shakespearean scepticism in philosophy today, and little, if any, in Shakespearean circles. Does this mean that Cavell's reading and interpreting are conspicuously his own to the degree that they are idiosyncratic? His readings have certainly been influential and they have enriched the public's understanding of the plays. However, it remains a rather closed loop: as far as I know, no new readings have taken his as their starting-points. This may, however, be more informative of the nature of academic literary interpretation than of the importance of Cavell's readings. Both literary scholars and philosophers have had their understandings both of the cultural phenomenon of scepticism, and the philosophical problem of scepticism, enhanced.

According to Cavell, the presence of the sceptical thematic in Shakespeare's plays was a question of scepticism being dormant in and tormenting the culture of the time. Do his readings succeed in unsettling the matter of priority between philosophy and literature? It is hard to know what he means by this aspiration. If it is taken to mean that a philosophical interest may be used to generate insight into a problematic from literature, then his answer to the question is certainly 'yes'. He claims that the scepticism enacted in Descartes is already in full flight in the Shakespearean corpus, that scepticism was a theme in culture, an almost tangible aspect of existence.

In many ways, such a claim does not depend on whether or not Shakespeare was conscious of what he was doing, whether it is likely that he could have replied to a drinking-mate that he was now writing a sustained analysis of scepticism in human relationships. The most important and interesting aspect of Cavell's analysis is not the diagnosis of the culture of which Shakespeare was a part, but the understanding it can give us of how scepticism is not only a concern internal to philosophy, but a problem which is alive in the relationships between people, both fictional and real. His readings of Shakespeare's plays make us see the questions relating to scepticism in a light different from that shed by earlier accounts internal to philosophy. According to Cavell himself, Shakespeare's tragedies interpret and reinterpret the sceptical problematic.[44] This is no passive illustration of the sceptical position, but a way of taking it further to cover aspects of interpersonal relations that were not dreamt of in Descartes' philosophy.

Is Cavell's analysis of scepticism in Shakespeare's *King Lear* philosophy *in* literature, or philosophy *through* literature? This is a distinction drawn by Stein Haugom Olsen and Peter Lamarque in their book *Truth, Fiction and Literature: A Philosophical Perspective*.[45] We can be said to have a case of philosophy *in* literature when 'a theme that is also the object of philosophical deliberation is given literary interpretation in terms of an imaginative world artistically constructed'. Philosophy *through* literature is when literary forms are used to communicate philosophical content which has already been worked out.[46] The latter, in other words, is when a philosopher writes a literary work to illustrate what he or she has already concluded as a philosopher. The former is when literature and philosophy share common problems, but pursue them in different ways. I think Cavell sees Shakespeare to have pursued philosophy in literature, and Cavell's readings do not just illustrate an argument. The inherent qualities of literature are necessary parts of the thematic Cavell identifies. Character, symbol and action are intrinsic elements of the philosophical import of the plays to a degree, and of a nature, other kinds of example could not furnish.

Can the same be said of Plato's *Phaedrus*? We saw in Chapter 6 that this dialogue is much like a modern play, and that a major aspect of the philosophical content of the dialogue relies also on our perception of the two characters who are present throughout. The beauty of Socrates' second speech, and other examples of Plato's consummate writerly skills, may suggest that this is philosophy *in* literature, that the themes of skilfully addressing the public, of the merits of writing and speaking, and the nature of soul, have been given a literary way of being worked out. On the other hand, much points to the second possibility, that independently conceived solutions to philosophical and rhetorical problems have found a literary form of being communicated, and that Plato's dialogues are indeed philosophy through forms which we today associate with literature. Perhaps this also indicates that the distinction between philosophy *in* and philosophy *through* literature is not as clear cut as Olsen and Lamarque seem to assume. Philosophy was not established as a separate discourse when Plato wrote, and in order to communicate a pursuit of truth he had to make use of the writerly forms known to his public, but he used those forms in ways designed to instigate philosophical processes. So despite a similarity in form between Plato and Shakespeare here, they are likely to be in pursuit of different goals.

Literary works are often complex constructions requiring close attention, and the discussion in this chapter shows that it is very difficult indeed to propose a single simple answer to how literature may contribute to the understanding of questions often considered philosophical. In any case, the issue calls for answers in the plural. Martha Nussbaum's view of how some literary works should be a necessary part of moral philosophy has been shown to lack sufficient attention to the dynamics of literary interpretation (our topic in Chapter 5), and the view that literature should destablilise our settled modes of thought, here associated with Bernard Harrison and Franz Kafka, was too narrow to do justice to the wide variety of literary works. Cavell's readings of Shakespeare's plays, though, show how literary and philosophical works share a concern for the same fundamental questions of human life. His own approach shows a keen attention to the interpretation of the literary texts, and a sensitivity to the philosophical issues involved. By engaging in literary interpretation as a philosophical activity he does not blur the distinctions between philosophy and literature so much as to show that engagement with literature as well as engagement with philosophy are aspects of 'the examined life'.

FURTHER READING

On Stanley Cavell and his diverse yet united writings on literature, film and various topics in philosophy, Stephen Mulhall has written a book: Stephen Mulhall, *Stanley Cavell: Philosophy's Recounting of the Ordinary* (Oxford: Clarendon, 1994), and he has also edited a useful collection of Cavell's writings: *The Cavell Reader* (Oxford: Blackwell, 1996).

A collection of articles on how modern political and ethical theory can be enriched through an engagement with works of literature: John Horton and Andrea T. Baumeister (eds), *Literature and the Political Imagination* (London: Routledge, 1996).

Richard Posner's attack on Martha Nussbaum's view of literature and philosophy, 'Against Ethical Criticism', *Philosophy and Literature*, 21 (1997), pp. 1–27, was answered by both Nussbaum and Wayne C. Booth, with a reply from Posner, in *Philosophy and Literature*, 22 (1998), pp. 343–412.

NOTES

1. Jostein Gaarder, *Sophie's World: A Novel about the History of Philosophy*, trans. Paulette Møller (London: Phoenix, 1995).
2. Martha C. Nussbaum, *Love's Knowledge: Essays on Philosophy and Literature* (Oxford: Oxford University Press, 1990), p. 5.
3. Nussbaum, *Love's Knowledge*, p. 12.
4. Nussbaum, *Love's Knowledge*, pp. 8–9.
5. Nussbaum, *Love's Knowledge*, p. 9.
6. Martha C. Nussbaum, 'Exactly and Responsibly: A Defense of Ethical Criticism', *Literature and Philosophy*, 22 (1998), pp. 343–65 (344).
7. Nussbaum, *Love's Knowledge*, p. 9.
8. Nussbaum, *Love's Knowledge*, p. 9.
9. Richard A. Posner, 'Against Ethical Criticism', *Literature and Philosophy*, 21 (1997), pp. 1–27 (21).
10. The emphases are mine, and both quotations are from *Love's Knowledge*, p. 23.
11. Nussbaum, *Love's Knowledge*, p. 23.
12. Posner, 'Against Ethical Criticism', p. 7.
13. A collection of papers debating the canon can be found in Robert van Hallberg (ed.), *Canons* (Chicago, IL: University of Chicago Press, 1984).
14. Martha C. Nussbaum, 'Exactly and Responsibly: A Defense of Ethical Criticism', *Philosophy and Literature*, 22 (1998), pp. 343–65 (348–49). This article is her defence against Posner's attacks on her position in the same journal (see note 9).
15. Martha C. Nussbaum, 'Flawed Crystals: James's *The Golden Bowl* and Literature as Moral Philosophy', in *Love's Knowledge: Essays on Philosophy and Literature* (Oxford: Oxford University Press, 1990), pp. 125–47. Posner, 'Against Ethical Criticism'.

16. Nussbaum, *Love's Knowledge*, pp. 134–5.
17. Nussbaum, *Love's Knowledge*, p. 47.
18. Peter Lamarque and Stein Haugom Olsen, *Truth, Ficiton and Literature: A Philosophical Perspective* (Oxford: Clarendon, 1994), p. 391.
19. The chapter in Lamarque and Haugom Olsen called 'Literature as Philosophy', pp. 386–97, also contains a criticism of Nussbaum's views.
20. See Chapter 4 of this book.
21. Helen Vendler, 'The Booby Trap', *New Republic*, October 7, 1996, pp. 34–7.
22. Peter Brooks, *Reading for the Plot: Design and Intention in Narrative* (New York: Vintage Books, 1984), p. 3. Quoted by Richard Eldridge, *On Moral Personhood: Philosophy, Literature, Criticism and Self-Understanding* (Chicago, IL: University of Chicago Press), p. 11.
23. Paul Ricoeur, 'Life in Quest of Narrative', in David Wood (ed.), *On Paul Ricoeur: Narrative and Interpretation* (London: Routledge, 1991), pp. 20–33, Alasdair MacIntyre, *After Virtue: A Study in Moral Theory* (London: Duckworth, 1981) and Charles Taylor, *Sources of the Self: The Making of the Modern Identity* (Cambridge: Cambridge University Press, 1989).
24. Richard Eldridge, *On Moral Personhood*.
25. Eldridge, *On Moral Personhood*, p. 12.
26. Eldridge, *On Moral Personhood*, p. 22.
27. Eldridge, *On Moral Personhood*, pp. 11 & 12.
28. Aristotle, *Nicomachean Ethics*, 1109b23. Nussbaum's translation, given in *The Fragility of Goodness: Luck and Ethics in Greek Tragedy and Philosophy* (Cambridge: Cambridge University Press, 1986), p. 300.
29. K. K. Ruthven, *Critical Assumptions* (Cambridge: Cambridge University Press, 1979), p. 184.
30. Nussbaum, 'Exactly and Responsibly: A Defense of Ethical Criticism', *Literature and Philosophy*, 22 (1998), pp. 343–65 (p. 353).
31. John Horton, 'Life, Literature and Ethical Theory', in John Horton and Andrea T. Baumeister (eds), *Literature and the Political Imagination* (London: Routledge, 1996), pp. 70–97 (p. 86).
32. Nussbaum, *Love's Knowledge*, p. 15.
33. Nussbaum, *Love's Knowledge*, p. 6.
34. Posner, 'Against Ethical Criticism', p. 18.
35. Franz Kafka, Letter to Oskar Pollak, 27 January 1904, in *Letters to Friends, Family, and Editors*, trans. Richard and Clara Winston (New York: Schocken Books, 1977), p. 16.
36. Bernard Harrison, *Inconvenient Fictions: Literature and the Limits of Theory* (New Haven, CT: Yale University Press, 1991), p. 11. He also advises that the place to look for great truths is not in novels but in physics texts (also p. 11).
37. His book *The World Viewed: Reflections on the Ontology of Film* (New York: Viking Press, 1971) is one of the classics of its genre.

38. Stanley Cavell, *Disowning Knowledge: In Six Plays of Shakespeare* (Cambridge: Cambridge University Press, 1987).
39. Cavell, *Disowning Knowledge*, p. 1.
40. Stanley Cavell, *The Claim of Reason: Wittgenstein, Skepticism, Morality, and Tragedy* (Oxford: Oxford University Press, 1979), p. xix.
41. Cavell, *Disowning Knowledge*, p. 85.
42. Cavell, *Disowning Knowledge*, p. 81.
43. Cavell, *Disowning Knowledge*, p. 1.
44. Cavell, *Disowning Knowledge*, p. 3.
45. Peter Lamarque and Stein Haugom Olsen, *Truth, Fiction and Literature*, p. 391.
46. These definitions from Lamarque and Haugom Olsen, *Truth, Fiction and Literature*, p. 391.

EIGHT

PHILOSOPHY/LITERATURE

The ancient animosity between philosophy and literature was based on rival claims to the same territory, and in recent years we have witnessed a growing acceptance of the mixed habitation of this territory. Just as Plato and others wanted to banish literature because of its appeal to the emotions beyond the control of rationality, so recent contributions to the debate have sought literature's return just because its genres manage to engage the emotions. Philosophy's self-image has often been that of the custodian of pure rationality, and the form and style of written philosophy has more or less consciously tried to reflect this. Given this picture, some have seen it as ironic that Plato should have adopted so many of the forms and tropes of the kind of writing he so thoroughly criticised. However, philosophy also has to communicate, as the discussion between Socrates and Phaedrus in the dialogue bearing the latter's name shows: one has to address those one wishes to convince in ways and forms suitable to the purpose.

Those purposes can be diverse, as we saw in our study of the writing of three different philosophers in Chapter 6. To at least two of those philosophers, Plato and Wittgenstein, it would be very difficult to respond in the same style and manner. These texts seem much more likely to have been written to provoke or entice readers to continue the discussions or investigations on their own parts, than to instruct and prove. This, incidentally, is also how literary works can function in relation to philosophy. Stanley Cavell's interpretations of the Shakespearean tragedies have become the focus for discussion and debate, unsettling any notion of a priority between philosophy and literature.

But what are philosophy and literature, then, are they just overlapping concepts too hazy to distinguish? We should be wary both of collapsing any distinction between philosophy and literature, and of distinguishing too sharply between them. Derrida, ironically, does both. By establishing a supposed opposition between philosophy and literature which is based on an opposition between language which is metaphorical, for literature, and pure and literal, for philosophy, it is easy to show that the latter opposition is not warranted and that therefore both oppositions collapse. But to resist tidy looking dichotomies is not to deny the existence of important distinctions.

There are, no doubt, those who will be frustrated with the lack of exception-free definitions and a neatly ordered conceptual field in this book. For such I can only recommend an attentive reading of Shakespeare's *King Lear*, and a study of Stanley Cavell's interpretation of the play. The desire for full and absolute knowledge, and its inherent disappointments, are facts of life. A life, moreover, which may be enhanced by the study of philosophy and literature.

BIBLIOGRAPHY

Åhlberg, Lars-Olof, and Tommie Zaine (eds), *Aesthetic Matters* (Uppsala: Enheten för Kulturstudier, Uppsala University, Sweden, 1994).

Aristotle, *Poetics: With the 'Tractatus Coislinianus', Reconstruction of 'Poetics II', and the Fragments of the 'On Poets'*, trans. Richard Janko (Indianapolis, IN: Hackett, 1987).

— *On Rhetoric: A Theory of Civic Discourse*, trans. George A. Kennedy (New York: Oxford University Press, 1991).

— *Nicomachean Ethics*, trans. Terence Irwin (Indianapolis, IN: Hackett, 1987).

— *The Politics*, trans. T. A. Sinclair, revised edn (London: Penguin, 1992).

Auerbach, Erich, *Mimesis: The Representation of Reality in Western Literature*, trans. Willard R. Trask (Princeton, NJ: Princeton University Press, 1953).

Augustine, *Confessions*, trans. R. S. Pine-Coffin (Harmondsworth: Penguin, 1961).

Barish, Jonas, *The Anti-Theatrical Prejudice* (Berkeley, CA: University of California Press, 1981).

Barker, Andrew, and Martin Warner, (eds), *The Language of the Cave*, *Apeiron* Special Issue (Edmonton, Alberta: Academic Printing and Publishing, 1992).

Barnes, Jonathan (ed.), *The Cambridge Companion to Aristotle* (Cambridge: Cambridge University Press, 1995).

Barthes, Roland, 'To Write: An Intransitive Verb?', in Richard Macksey and Eugenio Donato (eds), *The Structuralist Controversy: The Languages of Criticism and the Sciences of Man* (Baltimore, MD: Johns Hopkins University Press, 1972), p. 134–45.

— *Image-Music-Text*, trans. Stephen Heath (London: Fontana, 1977).

Baumgarten, Alexander Gottlieb, *Theoretische Ästhetik: Die grundlegenden Abschnitte der 'Aesthetica'*, H. R. Schweizer (ed.) (Hamburg: Felix Meiner Verlag, 1983).

— *Texte zur Grundlegung der Ästhetik*, ed. H. R. Schweizer (Hamburg: Felix Meiner Verlag, 1983).

Baxandall, Lee (ed.), *Radical Perspectives in the Arts* (Harmondsworth: Penguin, 1972).

Beardsley, Monroe C., *Aesthetics: Problems in the Philosophy of Criticism* (New York: Harcourt, Brace & World, 1958).

— 'The Authority of the Text', in Gary Iseminger (ed.), *Intention and Interpretation* (Philadelphia, PA: Temple University Press, 1992), pp. 24–40.

Belhassen, S., 'Aimé Césaire's A Tempest', in Lee Baxandall (ed.), *Radical Perspectives in the Arts* (Harmondsworth: Penguin, 1972), pp. 175–7.

Berkeley, George, *Three Dialogues between Hylas and Philonous*, Jonathan Dancy (ed.), (Oxford: Oxford *University Press, 1998)*.

Berry, Ralph (ed.), *On Directing Shakespeare* (London: Croom Helm, 1970).

Booth, Wayne C., *The Company We Keep: An Ethics of Fiction* (Berkeley, CA: University of California Press, 1988).

— 'Why Banning Ethical Criticism is a Serious Mistake', *Philosophy and Literature*, 22 (1998), pp. 366–93.

Bradford, Richard (ed.), *The State of Theory* (London: Routledge, 1993).

Brooks, Peter, *Reading for the Plot: Design and Intention in Narrative* (New York: Vintage Books, 1984).

Cascardi, Anthony J. (ed.), *Literature and the Question of Philosophy* (Baltimore, MD: Johns Hopkins University Press, 1987).

Cavell, Stanley, *Must We Mean What We Say?: A Book of Essays* (Cambridge: Cambridge University Press 1976) [1969].

— *The World Viewed: Reflections on the Ontology of Film* (New York: Viking Press, 1971).

— *The Claim of Reason: Wittgenstein, Skepticism, Morality, and Tragedy* (Oxford: Oxford University Press, 1979).

— *Disowning Knowledge: In Six Plays of Shakespeare* (Cambridge: Cambridge University Press, 1987).

— *In Quest of the Ordinary: Lines of Skepticism and Romanticism* (Chicago, IL: University of Chicago Press, 1988).

Coghill, Nevill, 'Sweeney Agonistes', in Tambimuttu & Richard Mach (eds), *T.S. Eliot: A Symposium* (London: Frank & Cass, 1965), pp. 82–7.

Conrad, Joseph, *Youth, Heart of Darkness, The End of the Tether*, Robert Kimbrough (ed.), (Oxford: Oxford University Press, 1984).

Cooper, David E. (ed.) *A Companion to Aesthetics* (Oxford: Blackwell, 1992).

Danto, Arthur C., 'Philosophy and/as/of Literature', in Anthony J. Cascardi (ed.) *Literature and the Question of Philosophy* (Baltimore, MD: Johns Hopkins University Press, 1987), pp. 3–23.

Davenant, Sir William, and John Dryden, 'The Tempest, or, The Enchanted Island: A Comedy', in Maximillian E. Novak (ed.), *The Works of John Dryden*, vol. 10, textual ed. Robert Guffey (Berkeley, CA: University of California Press, 1970), pp. 1–103.

Davidson, Donald, 'A Nice Derangement of Epitaphs', in Ernest LePore (ed.), *Truth and Interpretation: Perspectives on the Philosophy of Donald Davidson* (Oxford: Blackwell, 1986), pp. 433–46.

Davies, Philip R., *In Search of 'Ancient Israel'*, *Journal for the Study of the Old*

Testament, Supplement Series 148 (Sheffield: Sheffield Academic Press, 1992).

Dennett, Daniel, 'The Milk of Human Intentionality', *Behavioural and Brain Sciences*, 3 (1980), pp. 428–30.

— *Elbow Room* (Oxford: Oxford University Press, 1984).

Dennett, Daniel and Douglas R. Hofstadter (eds), *The Mind's I: Fantasies and Reflections on Mind and Soul* (New York: Basic Books, 1981).

Derrida, Jaques, *Of Grammatology*, trans. Gayatri C. Spivak (Baltimore, MD: Johns Hopkins University Press, 1976) [1967].

— *Writing and Difference*, trans. Alan Bass (London: Routledge, 1978) [1967].

— *Dissemination*, trans. Barbara Johnson (London: Athlone Press, 1981) [1972].

— *Margins of Philosophy*, trans. Alan Bass (Brighton: Harvester Press, 1982) [1972].

Donovan, Josephine (ed.), *Feminist Literary Criticism: Explorations in Theory* (Lexington, KY: University Press of Kentucky, 1975).

Dover, Kenneth J., *Greek Homosexuality* (London: Duckworth, 1978).

Easthope, Anthony, 'Paradigm Lost and Paradigm Regained', in Richard Bradford (ed.), *The State of Theory* (London: Routledge, 1993), pp. 90–104.

Eco, Umberto, *The Role of The Reader: Explorations in The Semiotics of Texts* (London: Hutchinson, 1979).

— *The Name of the Rose* (London: Secker & Warburg, 1983).

— *The Open Work*, trans. Anna Cancogeni (London: Hutchinson Radius, 1989) [1962].

— *The Limits of Interpretation* (Bloomington, IN: Indiana University Press, 1990).

Eco, Umberto, with Christine Brook-Rose, Jonathan Culler and Richard Rorty, Stefan Collini (ed.), *Interpretation and Overinterpretation* (Cambridge: Cambridge University Press, 1992).

Eldridge, Richard, *On Moral Personhood: Philosophy, Literature, Criticism, and Self-Understanding* (Chicago, IL: University of Chicago Press, 1989).

Ferrari, G. R. F., *Listening to the Cicadas: A Study of Plato's 'Phaedrus'* (Cambridge: Cambridge University Press, 1987).

— 'Plato and Poetry', in George A. Kennedy (ed.), *The Cambridge History of Literary Criticism: Volume 1 – Classical Criticism* (Cambridge: Cambridge University Press, 1989), pp. 92–148.

Foucault, Michel, *Discipline and Punish: The Birth of the Prison*, trans. Alan Sheridan (London: Allen Lane, 1977).

— *The History of Sexuality*, 3 vols, trans. Robert Hurley (Harmondsworth: Penguin, 1984–88).

— 'What is an Author?', in Paul Rabinow (ed.), *The Foucault Reader* (Harmondsworth: Penguin, 1984) pp. 101–20.

Gaarder, Jostein, *Sophie's World: A Novel about the History of Philosophy*, trans. Paulette Møller (London: Phoenix, 1995).

Gabel, John B. and Charles B. Wheeler, *The Bible as Literature: An Introduction* (New York: Oxford University Press, 1986).

Gadamer, Hans-Georg, *Wahrheit und Methode: Grundzüge Einer Philosophischen Hermeneutik*, Gesammelte Werke, Band 1, Sechste Auflage (Tübingen: J. C. B. Mohr, 1990).

— *Truth and Method*, John Cumming and Garrett Barden (eds), trans. William Glen-Doepel, from the 2nd German edn (1965) of *Wahrheit und Methode*, 2nd English edn (London: Sheed and Ward, 1979).

— *Philosophical Hermeneutics*, David E. Linge (ed. and trans.) (Berkeley, CA: University of California Press, 1976).

Gallie, W. B., 'Essentially Contested Concepts', *Proceedings of the Aristotelian Society* 56 (1955–56), pp. 167–98.

— *Philosophy and the Historical Understanding* (London: Chatto & Windus, 1964).

Gould, Thomas, *The Ancient Quarrel Between Poetry and Philosophy* (Princeton, NJ: Princeton, 1991).

Griffiths, A. Phillips (ed.), *Philosophy and Literature*, Royal Institute of Philosophy Lecture Series, 16 (Cambridge: Cambridge University Press, 1984).

Hallberg, Robert van (ed.), *Canons* (Chicago, IL: University of Chicago Press, 1984).

Halliwell, Stephen, 'Aristotle's Poetics', in George A. Kennedy (ed.), *The Cambridge History of Literary Criticism: Volume 1 – Classical Criticism* (Cambridge: Cambridge University Press, 1989), pp. 149–83.

Hare, R. M., *Moral Thinking* (Oxford: Oxford University Press, 1981).

Harrison, Bernard, *Inconvenient Fictions: Literature and the Limits of Theory* (New Haven, CT: Yale University Press, 1991).

Heidegger, Martin, *Being and Time*, trans. John Macquarrie and Edward Robinson (Oxford: Blackwell, 1962).

Hellesnes, Jon, *Carolus, klovnen: Roman* (Oslo: Gyldendal, 1982).

Hirsch, E. D., jr., *Validity in Interpretation* (New Haven, CT: Yale University Press, 1967).

— *The Aims of Interpretation* (Chicago, IL: University of Chicago Press, 1976).

Hogan, Charles Beecher, *Shakespeare in the Theatre 1701–1800: A Record of Performances in London 1701–1750* (Oxford: Clarendon, 1952).

Horden, Peregrine (ed.), *The Novelist as Philosopher: Modern Fiction and the History of Ideas*, The Chichele Lectures, 1982 (Oxford: All Souls College, 1982).

Horton, John, and Andrea T. Baumeister (eds), *Literature and the Political Imagination* (London: Routledge, 1996).

Horton, John, 'Life, Literature and Ethical Theory', in Andrea John Horton and T. Baumeister (eds), *Literature and the Political Imagination* (London: Routledge, 1996), pp. 70–97.

Hoy, David Couzens, *The Critical Circle: Literature and History in Contemporary Hermeneutics* (Berkeley, CA: University of California Press, 1978).

Hume, David, *Dialogues Concerning Natural Religion*, N. Kemp Smith (ed.) (London: Nelson, 1947).

Ingarden, Roman, *The Literary Work of Art: An Investigation on the Borderlines of Ontology, Logic, and Theory of Literature*, trans. George G. Grabowicz (Evanston, IL: Northwestern University Press, 1973).

— *The Cognition of the Literary Work of Art*, trans. Ruth Ann Crowly and Kenneth R. Olsen (Evanston, IL: Northwestern University Press, 1973).

Iseminger, Gary (ed.), *Intention and Interpretation* (Philadelphia, PA: Temple University Press, 1992).

Judovitz, Dalia, 'Philosophy and Poetry: The Difference Between Them in Plato and Descartes', in Anthony J. Cascardi (ed.), *Literature and the Question of Philosophy* (Baltimore, MD: Johns Hopkins UP, 1987), pp. 26–51.

Kafka, Franz, *Letters to Friends, Family, and Editors*, trans. Richard and Clara Winston (New York: Schocken Books, 1977).

Kant, Immanuel, *The Critique of Judgement*, trans. Werner S. Pluhar (Indianapolis, IN: Hackett, 1987) [1790].

Keesey, Donald (ed.), *Contexts For Criticism*, 3rd edn (Mountain View, CA: Mayfield Publishing, 1998).

Kekes, John, 'Essentially Contested Concepts: A Reconsideration', *Philosophy and Rhetoric*, 10 (1977), pp. 71–89.

Kennedy, George A. (ed.), *The Cambridge History of Literary Criticism: Volume 1 – Classical Criticism* (Cambridge: Cambridge University Press, 1989).

Kermode, Frank, *The Genesis of Secrecy: On the Interpretation of Narrative* (Cambridge, MA: Harvard University Press, 1979).

Kierkegaard, Søren, *Either/Or*, Howard V. Hong and Edna H. Hong (ed. and trans.), vol. 3–4, in *Kierkegaard's Writings*, general editor Howard V. Hong (Princeton, NJ: Princeton University Press, 1987).

Kraut, Richard (ed.), *The Cambridge Companion to Plato* (Cambridge: Cambridge University Press, 1992).

Lamarque, Peter, 'The Death of the Author: An Analytical Autopsy', *British Journal of Aesthetics*, 30 (1990), pp. 319–31.

— *Fictional Points of View* (Ithaca, IN: Cornell University Press, 1996).

Lamarque, Peter, and Stein Haugom Olsen, *Truth, Fiction and Literature: A Philosophical Perspective* (Oxford: Clarendon, 1994).

Lang, Berel, *Philosophy and the Art of Writing: Studies in Philosophical and Literary Style* (Lewisburg: Bucknell University Press, 1983).

— *The Anatomy of Philosophical Style: Literary Philosophy and the Philosophy of Literature* (Oxford: Blackwell, 1990).

Lear, Jonathan, 'Katharsis', in Amélie Oksenberg Rorty (ed.), *Essays on Aristotle's Poetics* (Princeton, NJ: Princeton University Press, 1992), pp. 315–40.

LePore, Ernest (ed.), *Truth and Interpretation: Perspectives on the Philosophy of Donald Davidson* (Oxford: Blackwell, 1986).

Lessing, Doris, 'To Room Nineteen', in M. H. Abrams (general ed.), *The Norton Anthology of English Literature*, 6th edn, vol. 2 (New York: Norton, 1993), pp. 2300–23.

— *The Sirian Experiments* (London: Granada, 1982).

Levin, Richard, *New Readings vs. Old Plays* (Chicago, IL: University of Chicago Press, 1979).

Lodge, David (ed.), *20th Century Literary Criticism: A Reader* (London: Longman, 1972).

— (ed.), *Modern Criticism and Theory: A Reader* (London: Longman, 1988).

Lyotard, Jean-François, *The Post-Modern Condition: A Report on Knowledge*, trans. Geoff Bennington and Brian Massumi (Manchester: Manchester University Press, 1984) [1979].

MacIntyre, Alasdair, *After Virtue: A Study in Moral Theory* (London: Duckworth, 1981).

Macksey, Richard, and Eugenio Donato (eds), *The Structuralist Controversy: The Languages of Criticism and the Sciences of Man* (Baltimore, MD: Johns Hopkins University Press, 1972).

Man, Paul de, 'The Resistance to Theory', in David Lodge (ed.), *Modern Criticism and Theory: A Reader* (London: Longman, 1988), pp. 355–71.

Manguel, Alberto, *A History of Reading* (London: Flamingo, 1997).

Mason, Jeff, *Philosophical Rhetoric: The Function of Indirection in Philosophical Writing* (Routledge: London, 1989).

Miller, Jonathan, in Ralph Berry (ed.), *On Directing Shakespeare* (London: Croom Helm, 1970).

Montaigne, Michel de, *Essays*, trans. J. M. Cohen (Harmondsworth: Penguin, 1958).

Mulhall, Stephen, *Stanley Cavell: Philosophy's Recounting of the Ordinary* (Oxford: Clarendon, 1994).

— (ed.), *The Cavell Reader* (Oxford: Blackwell, 1996).

Mundle, C. W. K., *A Critique of Linguistic Philosophy* (Oxford: Oxford University Press, 1970).

Murdoch, Iris, *The Sovereignty of Good* (London: Routledge, 1970).

— *The Black Prince* (London: Chatto & Windus, 1973).

— *The Fire and the Sun: Why Plato Banished the Artists* (Oxford: Oxford University Press, 1977).

— *The Sea, The Sea* (London: Chatto & Windus, 1978).

— *The Philosopher's Pupil* (London: Chatto & Windus, 1983).

— *Metaphysics as a Guide to Morals* (London: Chatto & Windus, 1992).

Murray, Penelope, 'Inspiration and *Mimesis* in Plato', in Andrew Barker and Martin Warner (eds), *The Language of the Cave*, *Apeiron* Special Issue (Edmonton, Alberta: Academic Printing and Publishing, 1992), pp. 27–46.

Nagel, Thomas, *Mortal Questions* (Cambridge: Cambridge University Press, 1979).

Nehamas, Alexander, 'Plato and the Mass Media', *The Monist*, 71 (1988), pp. 214–34.

Nietzsche, Friedrich, *Thus Spoke Zarathustra: A Book for Everyone and No One*, trans. R. J. Hollingdale (Harmondsworth: Penguin, 1969).

Nilan, Mary M., '*The Tempest* at the Turn of the Century: Cross-Currents in Production', *Shakespeare Survey*, 25 (1972), pp. 113–23.

Norris, Christopher, *Deconstruction: Theory and Practice* (London: Methuen, 1982).

— *Derrida* (London: Fontana, 1987).

— *Truth and the Ethics of Criticism* (Manchester: Manchester University Press, 1995).

— *Reclaiming Truth* (London: Lawrence and Wishart, 1996).

— *Against Relativism: Philosophy of Science, Deconstruction and Critical Theory* (Oxford: Blackwell, 1997).

Nussbaum, Martha C., *The Fragility of Goodness: Luck and Ethics in Greek Tragedy and Philosophy* (Cambridge: Cambridge University Press, 1986).

— *Love's Knowledge: Essays on Philosophy and Literature* (Oxford: Oxford University Press, 1990).

— *Poetic Justice: The Literary Imagination and Public Life* (Boston, MA: Beacon Press, 1995).

— 'Exactly and Responsibly: A Defense of Ethical Criticism', *Philosophy and Literature*, 22 (1998), pp. 343–65.

Oakeshott, Michael, 'The Voice of Poetry in the Conversation of Mankind', in *Rationalism in Politics and Other Essays* (Indianapolis, IN: Liberty Press, 1991), pp. 488–541.

Olsen, Stein Haugom, *The Structure of Literary Understanding* (Cambridge: Cambridge University Press, 1978).

— 'Thematic Concepts: Where Philosophy Meets Literature', in A. Phillips Griffiths (ed.) *Philosophy and Literature*, Royal Institute of Philosophy Lecture Series, 16 (Cambridge: Cambridge University Press, 1984) pp. 75–93.

— *The End of Literary Theory* (Cambridge: Cambridge University Press, 1987).

— 'The Role of Theory in Literary Studies', in *Aesthetic Matters*, Lars-Olof Åhlberg and Tommie Zaine (eds) (Uppsala: Enheten för Kulturstudier, Uppsala University, Sweden, 1994), pp. 101–13.

Olsen, Stein Haugom, and Peter Lamarque, *Truth, Fiction and Literature: A Philosophical Perspective* (Oxford: Clarendon, 1994).

Palmer, Frank, *Literature and Moral Understanding* (Oxford: Clarendon, 1992).

Picard-Cambridge, Arthur, *The Theatre of Dionysus in Athens* (Oxford: Clarendon Press, 1946).

— *The Dramatic Festivals of Athens*, 2nd edition (Oxford: Clarendon Press, 1968).

Plato, *Phaedo*, trans. David Gallop (Oxford: Oxford University Press, 1975).

— *The Republic*, trans. Desmond Lee, 2nd edn (Harmondsworth: Penguin, 1974).

— *Phaedrus*, trans. R. Hackforth (Cambridge: Cambridge University Press, 1952).

— *Phaedrus*, trans. C. J. Rowe (Warminster: Aris and Phillips, 1986).

— *The Collected Works of Plato: Including the Letters*, Edith Hamilton and

Huntington Cairns (eds), Bollingen Series 71 (Princeton, NJ: Princeton University Press, 1989).

Posner, Richard A., 'Against Ethical Criticism', *Philosophy and Literature*, 21 (1997), pp. 1–27.

— 'Against Ethical Criticism: Part Two', *Philosophy and Literature*, 22 (1998), pp. 394–412.

Postman, Neil, *Amusing Ourselves to Death: Public Discourse in the Age of Show Business* (New York: Viking Press, 1985).

Quine, Willard van Orman, *From a Logical Point of View* (Cambridge, MA: Harvard University Press, 1953).

— *The Time of My Life* (Cambridge, MA: MIT Press, 1985).

Quine, Willard van Orman, with J. S. Ullian, *The Web of Belief* (New York: Random House, 1970).

Rabinow, Paul, (ed.), *The Foucault Reader* (Harmondsworth: Penguin, 1984).

Ramberg, Bjørn T., *Donald Davidson's Philosophy of Language* (Oxford: Blackwell, 1989).

Register, Cheri, 'American Feminist Literary Criticism: A Bibliographical Introduction', in Josephine Donovan (ed.), *Feminist Literary Criticism: Explorations in Theory* (Lexington, KY: University Press of Kentucky, 1975), pp. 1–28.

Richards, I. A., *Principles of Literary Criticism* (London: Kegan Paul, 1926) [1924].

— *Practical Criticism: A Study of Literary Judgement* (London: Routledge, 1929).

Richards, I. A., and C. K. Ogden, *The Meaning of Meaning: A Study of the Influence of Language upon Thought and of the Science of Symbolism*, 3rd edn. (London: Kegan Paul, 1930) [1923].

Ricoeur, Paul, *Hermeneutics and The Human Sciences*, trans. John B. Thompson (Cambridge: Cambridge University Press, 1981).

— *Time and Narrative*, 3 vols, trans. K. McLaughlin and D. Pellauer (Chicago, IL: University of Chicago Press, 1984–88).

— 'Life in Quest of Narrative', in David Wood (ed.), *On Paul Ricoeur: Narrative and Interpretation* (London: Routledge, 1991), pp. 20–33

Robinson, Richard, *Definition* (Oxford: Clarendon Press, 1954).

Rorty, Amélie Oksenberg (ed.), *Essays on Aristotle's Poetics* (Princeton, NJ: Princeton University Press, 1992).

Rorty, Richard, *Consequences of Pragmatism (Essays: 1972–1980)* (Brighton: Harvester Press, 1982).

Rosen, Stanley, *Plato's Sophist: The Drama of Original and Image* (New Haven, CT: Yale University Press, 1983).

Ruthven, K. K., *Critical Assumptions* (Cambridge: Cambridge University Press, 1979).

Sacks, Oliver, *The Man Who Mistook His Wife for a Hat* (London: Picador, 1986).

Sartre, Jean-Paul, *Nausea*, trans. R. Baldick (Harmondsworth: Penguin, 1965).

Saussure, Ferdinand de, *Course in General Linguistics*, eds Charles Bally, Albert Sechehaye and Albert Reidlinger, trans. Wade Baskin (London: Peter Owen, 1960) [1915].

Savile, Anthony, *The Test of Time: An Essay in Philosophical Aesthetics* (Oxford: Clarendon Press, 1982).

Schaper, Eva, *Prelude to Aesthetics* (London: Allen and Unwin, 1968).

Shakespeare, William, *The Tempest*, Stephen Orgel (ed.) (Oxford: Oxford University Press, 1987).

Skilleås, Ole Martin, 'Anachronistic Themes and Literary Value: *The Tempest*', *British Journal of Aesthetics*, 31 (1991), pp. 122–33.

— 'Restraint in the Darkness', *English Studies*, 76 (1995), pp. 52–63.

— *Literature and the Value of Interpretation: The Cases of The Tempest and Heart of Darkness* (Bergen: Department of Philosophy, University of Bergen, 1996).

— 'The Critique of Writing in Plato's *Phaedrus*: A Meta-fictional Heuristic?', *Philosophical Writings*, 3 (1998), issue 8, pp. 3–13.

Sörbom, Göran, *Mimesis and Art: Studies in the Origin and Early Development of an Aesthetic Vocabulary* (Stockholm: Bonnier, 1966).

Stolnitz, Jerome, 'On the Origins of "Aesthetic Disinterestedness"', *Journal of Aesthetics and Art Criticism*, 20 (1961–62), pp. 131–43.

Strauss, Leo, *Persecution and the Art of Writing* (Chicago, IL: The University of Chicago Press, 1952).

Szlezák, Thomas A., *Reading Plato*, trans. G. Zanker (London: Routledge, 1999).

Tallis, Raymond, *Not Saussure: A Critique of Post-Saussurean Literary Theory* (London: Macmillan, 1988).

Tambimuttu, and Richard Mach (eds), *T. S. Eliot: A Symposium* (London: Frank & Cass, 1965).

Taylor, Charles, *Sources of the Self: The Making of the Modern Identity* (Cambridge: Cambridge University Press, 1989).

Tolstoy, Leo, *What is Art? and Essays on Art*, trans. Aylmer Maude (Oxford: Oxford University Press, 1930).

Vendler, Helen, 'The Booby Trap', *New Republic*, October 7, 1996, pp. 34–7.

Walcot, Peter, *Greek Drama in its Theatrical and Social Context* (Cardiff: University of Wales Press, 1976).

Ward, David, ' "Now I will believe there are unicorns": *The Tempest* and its Theatre', *English*, 36 (1987), pp. 95–110.

Warner, Martin, *Philosophical Finesse: Studies in the Art of Rational Persuasion* (Oxford: Clarendon Press, 1989).

— 'On Not Deconstructing the Difference Between Literature and Philosophy', *Philosophy and Literature*, 13 (1989), pp. 16–27.

— (ed.), *The Bible as Rhetoric* (London: Routledge, 1990).

— 'Literature, Truth and Logic', *Philosophy*, 74 (1999) pp. 29–54.

Warner, Martin, and Andrew Barker (eds), *The Language of the Cave*, *Apeiron* Special Issue (Edmonton, Alberta: Academic Printing and Publishing, 1992).

Warnke, Georgia, *Gadamer: Hermeneutics, Tradition and Reason* (Cambridge: Polity, 1987).

Weitz, Morris, *Philosophy in Literature: Shakespeare, Voltaire, Tolstoy, and Proust* (Detroit, MI: Wayne State University Press, 1963).

Wellek, René and Austin Warren, *Theory of Literature* (London: Jonathan Cape, 1949).

Williams, Bernard, *Shame and Necessity* (Berkeley, CA: University of California Press, 1993).

Wilson, Daniel, *Caliban: The Missing Link* (London: Macmillan, 1873).

Wimsatt, W. K., *The Verbal Icon: Studies in the Meaning of Poetry* (Lexington, KY: University Press of Kentucky, 1954).

Wimsatt, W. K., and Monroe C. Beardsley, 'The Intentional Fallacy', in David Lodge (ed.) *20th Century Literary Criticism: A Reader* (London: Longman, 1972), pp. 334–45.

— 'The Affective Fallacy', in David Lodge (ed.), *20th Century Literary Criticism: A Reader* (London: Longman, 1972), pp. 345–58.

Wittgenstein, Ludwig, *Tractatus Logico-Philosophicus*, trans. D. F. Pears and B. F. McGuinness (London: Routledge, 1961) [1921].

— *Philosophical Investigations*, trans. G. E. M. Anscombe (Oxford: Blackwell, 1953).

— *Culture and Value*, G. H. von Wright (ed.), trans. Peter Winch, revised edn of the text by Alois Pichler (Oxford: Blackwell, 1998).

Wood, David (ed.), *On Paul Ricoeur: Narrative and Interpretation* (London: Routledge, 1991).

INDEX